Extreme sports are interesting, but spor parents are sports extremists, pushing highly-competitive, high-travel soccer or basketball ... Some coaches are sports extremists, emphasizing winning at all costs ... Some athletes, even Christian ones, fall into the trap of glorifying themselves rather than God ... John Perritt's well-written look at stewardship in sports gets it right: *Time Out!* can show parents, coaches, and athletes how to use sports to win victories in life.

MARVIN OLASKY
Editor in Chief, World Magazine

Never have I read such a well-grounded, gospel-centered critique of youth sports culture as it exists today. By no means does John Perritt lead us to view sports as bad. Quite the opposite in fact, as sports in its proper place is a good gift of God to his children. But through the lenses of stewardship John challenges us to reevaluate the effects on our families, calendar, money and worship when sports are elevated to the degree they are now. While a difficult reality to face, I hope this book will spur us on to change for the betterment of our kids's souls, and to His glory.

KRISTEN HATTON
Author of *Exodus: The Gospel-Centered Life for Students, Face Time: Your Identity in a Selfie World* and *Get Your Story Straight*

Time Out! is a wildly relevant and deeply compelling look at one of the greatest cultural phenomena of our day: sports. As teenagers (and those who love them) try to navigate this complex issue, John Perritt steps in with gracious counsel. He is exceptionally empathetic yet unflinchingly honest and uncompromisingly biblical. I believe this book will spur many teens and their families to find more joy in sports as they find ultimate satisfaction in the Creator of sports.

JAQUELLE CROWE
Author of *This Changes Everything: How the Gospel Transforms the Teen Years*

John Perritt's new and timely book, *Time Out!*, helps start a broader and crucial conversation surrounding 'youth sports' … With clarity and clear theological insight, John unpacks and provides a balanced response to key issues, for example, performance-based identity, idolatry and neglect of family time, bible-study, prayer and church engagement due to 'packed' youth sports schedules. Importantly, the author also recognises the importance of celebrating sport as a gift and as a source of physical, emotional and spiritual well-being. This book will make you think more critically about 'youth sports', while still celebrating them as a God-given gift.

NICK J. WATSON

Associate Professor, Sport and Social Justice, York St John University, UK

One of the questions I receive most often from parents is, 'How much is too much for my children to be involved in sports?' This book doesn't offer easy solutions, but it does provide the wisdom that parents need to drive them to God's Word as they decide how sports can be used for God's glory in their children's lives.

TIMOTHY PAUL JONES

C. Edwin Gheens Endowed Chair of Christian Family Ministry,
The Southern Baptist Theological Seminary, Louisville, Kentucky

A case could be made that sport has become our #1 national obsession and diversion. From U5 to the pros, and from the field to the sidelines, we have turned sport from a good thing into an ultimate thing. If Jesus Christ is truly the Lord of all of life, then it's necessary for us to follow Him into the sphere of sport … playing, parenting, and spectating to His glory. John Perritt offers thoughtful Gospel-grounded guidance for how to engage with God's good gift of play.

WALT MUELLER

Author of *Youth Culture 101* and *Engaging the Soul of Youth
Culture: Bridging Teen Worldviews and Christian Truth*
President of Center for Parent/Youth Understanding

It takes someone who loves sports, both as a participant and a fan to be able to offer a biblically balanced and theologically informed view of how involvement in sports can affect our families. John brings the perspective of an experienced youth pastor who has seen both the benefits and the pitfalls of athletics as he seeks to help young people and their parents set wise priorities ... While celebrating the benefits of sports, he also provides biblical warnings.

JIM NEWHEISER

Director of the Christian Counseling Program and Associate Professor of Counseling and Practical Theology at Reformed Theological Seminary, Charlotte, North Carolina
Executive Director, IBCD (The Institute for Biblical Counseling and Discipleship)

After playing five seasons in the NFL and now serving in both pro and student ministry, I see how the sports world affects today's athlete. John Perritt accurately addresses the idolatrous nature of youth sports with a sobering yet redemptive perspective. He makes this topic accessible for all readers and I believe *Time Out!* is a must-read for parents, coaches, and youth leaders who care about properly equipping the next generation of athletes.

CASEY CRAMER

Fullback/Tight End, Tampa Bay Buccaneers, New York Jets, Tennessee Titans, Carolina Panthers, & Miami Dolphins (2004-2009)
NFL Chaplain, Tennessee Titans (current)
Pastor of Kids, Students, and Families of Christ Presbyterian Church, Nashville, Tennessee

Sports, salvation, sinners, and the saints. What in the world do they have to do with each other? This is what John Perritt writes about. And he does it in a very clear, biblical, and encouraging way. After all, biblically speaking, everything and everyone operates under the sovereign ruling and pre-appointed purposes of God. And this includes all sports.

ELIAS MEDEIROS

Harriet Barbour Professor of Missions, Reformed Theological Seminary

This book winsomely explores how the Gospel speaks to the many sticky issues and blatant idolatry of our sport-loving culture. Church, here is much needed help to pursue sports with biblical values! A sports fan himself, John engages us, as parents and coaches, with honest storytelling and gracious pastoral exhortation. The theological insights challenge us to see our sports experiences in light of God's Story: His good creation, people's rebellion, Jesus' provision of redemption, and God's promise of final restoration.

TASHA CHAPMAN
Author of *Resilient Ministry: What Pastors Told Us About Surviving and Thriving*
Professor of Educational Ministries, Covenant Theological Seminary,
St. Louis, Missouri

John Perritt has done something that I've failed to see anybody do – produce a biblical theology of youth sports and show how the Scriptures relate to the biblical principle of stewardship. With wit, wisdom, and exegesis, Perritt presents a deeper, more theologically-sound understanding of the world of athletics ... If you're involved or you have children involved in youth sports, this will be a helpful guide to thinking more biblically about it.

BRIAN H. COSBY
Author of *Giving Up Gimmicks:*
Reclaiming Youth Ministry from an Entertainment Culture

Teenagers, but especially the parents of teenagers, need to read this book ... Today, like never before, adults and teens live for sport, sacrifice for sport, travel for sport, devote their time, talents, and treasure to sport. The tragic consequence is that church has been displaced in many families punted to the sidelines by the central place our college team or our teenager's track meet has come to occupy in our hearts and on our calendars ... John Perritt shows us how to celebrate the beauty and goodness of sports as a gift of God's common grace without finding our identity in them.

DAVID STRAIN
Senior Pastor, The First Presbyterian Church, Jackson, Mississippi

If all of life for the believer is worship in a true sense, then here John Perritt helps us worship more faithfully by placing sport in its proper context of creation, fall, redemption, and glory! ... The unity, celebration, shared joy, and exhilaration of sport all point us back to what once was in the garden and will be one day again in fullness. Would you be a good steward of God's gift of sport?

CARL H. KALBERKAMP
Senior Pastor, Pear Orchard Presbyterian Church, Ridgeland, Mississippi

Many families unknowingly sign up for intense sports commitments and see their family lives disrupted and fragmented. This book provides a theology of sports that will give parents and coaches a means by which to think theologically about their kids' athletic activities. John's book offers a thought-provoking resource that will help parents search their hearts, discern God's will, and make wise choices for their whole family in the realm of kids' sports.

CAMERON COLE
Author of *Gospel-Centered Youth Ministry* and *Therefore I Have Hope:*
12 Truths that Comfort, Sustain, and Redeem in Tragedy
Director of Children, Youth, and Family at Cathedral Church of the Advent

It is with great heart and sincerity that John Perritt offers this challenge to the idolatry of youth sports. Wisely navigating both the glory and the depravity of our current cultural moment, he invites us to consider more thoughtful and intentional discipleship relating to their participation.

LIZ EDRINGTON
Coordinator of Young Adults at North Shore Fellowship
Counselor at Summit Counseling Center in Chattanooga, Tennessee

Every church engaging in sports ministry needs to have this book as a resource for setting clear and gospel-focused guidelines. Perritt has done a considerable service in addressing the key issues in short compass and providing biblical answers. Essential reading.

DEREK W. H. THOMAS
Senior Minister, First Presbyterian Church, Columbia, South Carolina
Chancellor's Professor, Reformed Theological Seminary
Teaching Fellow, Ligonier Ministries

This is a clear, concise and compassionate book that insightfully probes to the heart of an important issue in our day – a Christian attitude to youth sports. Sport is good but it is not God. Writing with sound biblical theology, vibrant illustrations, memorable quotes and helpful practical application, John Perritt has made a significant contribution to this topic. It's a must read!

GAVIN PEACOCK

Former professional footballer. Director of International Outreach for the Council on Biblical Manhood & Womanhood, pastor at Calvary Grace Church in Calgary, Alberta

Few activities incite as much attention, dedication, or obsession as sports. In fact, we could rightfully say that we live in a world captivated by sports. Therefore, it is important for Christians to possess a right view in this area of life. In steps John Perritt with a careful, practical and theological approach to our treasured recreations. John's reader will find the love of an athlete, the wisdom of an experienced pastor, and the sensitivity of a father in these pages.

JASON HELOPOULOS

Senior Pastor, University Reformed Church, East Lansing, Michigan

Like any of God's good gifts we must seek wisdom as we wholeheartedly engage athletics. Sports can be both adventurous and idolatrous. This tension needs thoughtful consideration and wisdom to navigate the competitive athletic lure and the demands of time on any family. Sports have the potential of disrupting our families, Christian community and love for the gospel. Therefore I recommend you read John's book to better understand the balance and strive to keep sports in a proper and biblical balance.

DAN DUMAS

CEO and Founder of Red Buffalo
Senior Vice President of the Southern Baptist Theological Seminary (2007-2017)

TIME OUT!

THE GIFT OR GOD OF YOUTH SPORTS

JOHN PERRITT

CHRISTIAN
FOCUS

Copyright © John Perritt 2018

paperback ISBN 978-1-5271-0177-7
epub ISBN 978-1-5271-0255-2
Mobi ISBN 978-1-5271-0256-9

10 9 8 7 6 5 4 3 2 1

Published in 2018
by
Christian Focus Publications Ltd.,
Geanies House, Fearn, Ross-shire,
IV20 1TW, Scotland, U.K.
www.christianfocus.com

Cover design by Daniel van Straaten
Printed by Bell and Bain, Glasgow

CONTENTS

FOREWORD

IN 2012 I walked away from the National Football League. It was a game that I had played twenty-three years of my life. People thought that I was crazy for walking away from a game that millions of people love, and millions of young men would give anything to play. But in 2008, when I truly came to know Christ, my eyes were opened to how much those same people not only love the game but in fact worship it.

For example: people will go to a high school football game on Friday night, wake up early to attend (or watch) college football all day Saturday, turn on the radio Sunday morning to listen to the pregame report, go tailgate for three hours, go to the game, get back in the car and listen to the postgame report, then get up on Monday morning to watch ESPN so that they can see the highlights of that same game. That is worship!

In *Time Out!*, John Perritt gives a biblical framework to think about God and sports. Which are we truly worshiping? It is a great exploration of both sides of the argument with a clear view of his position on the matter. He reminds us that Christian parents must take the discipleship of their children seriously and to be very vigilant in the messages that they are sending when choosing one over the other.

When I read this book, I thought of the age-old proverb; 'more is caught than taught.' And if I say that God is the most important thing yet consistently choose the sporting event over the things of God, which is truly more important? In our day and age of 'sports' I believe that it is vitally important for the Christian to heed the words of John and take what I believe to be a healthy and, more importantly, biblical position on God and sports. In some ways our children's souls could very well depend on it.

KELLY JENNINGS
Cornerback, Seattle Seahawks (2006-2010) and
Cincinnati Bengals (2011)

ACKNOWLEDGEMENTS

THIS book is really the culmination of many years serving in youth ministry combined with years invested on the athletic field. Being involved in multiple sports in the years of my youth birthed a great love for athletic competition. Now that I am a grown man and father, my perspective has shifted to see sports with a more discerning eye. As God has graciously grown me in my understanding of His Lordship, I've seen how foundational biblical stewardship is to being a follower of Christ.

In light of the above, I am very thankful to The Southern Baptist Theological Seminary for allowing me to pursue a deeper understanding in the area of stewardship of sports and adolescent spirituality. During my three years at SBTS, I was able to invest a great deal of writing and research in this area and am thankful they approved this topic as a possible thesis.

The finished product of this book is vastly improved from its initial form. Much of this is due to the editorial comments and scholarly advice of Dr. Timothy Paul Jones. It has been such a privilege to watch this project move from a concept to a completed work, which has taken place through innumerable conversations with Dr. Jones in person, over the phone, and email. The value of this work has been immensely improved by your assistance; thank you.

I would also like to thank Pear Orchard Presbyterian Church (POPC) for their loving, pastoral care they have given to me and my family throughout the years. I came on staff at the age of twenty-three with no children. I am now thirty-seven and have five children. You have watched me grow and have discipled me in numerous ways. Much of my thinking on this subject has developed because of the families I minister alongside. I thank God for the body of believers at POPC.

I want to thank Jackie Shelt for her edits that have made this work more polished. I'm so thankful the Lord moved in your heart to approach me about my possible editing needs. This work has much of your work in it.

I would also like to thank Pastors Carl, Caleb, John, and Emilio for the many discussions we've shared about youth sports. You each have sharpened and challenged my thinking in so many ways. This work bears much of your wisdom and thoughtfulness.

My parents, sister, and grandmother have offered so many words of encouragement throughout this process. I am so thankful for the gift each of you are to me and your faithful love throughout the years.

My wife, Ashleigh, you gave so much of your time watching the children in order for me to devote time to this work. Thank you for sacrificing time and energy to ensure I could focus myself on this work. To be quite candid, this work would not exist apart from you.

Lastly, I thank my beautiful Savior, Jesus Christ. It is out of a desire to more deeply understand Your Lordship, that this work was written. You are King of all creation and I pray that this work is honoring to You.

JOHN PERRITT
Ridgeland, Mississippi
November 2016

Better is open rebuke than hidden love.
Faithful are the wounds of a friend …

Proverbs 27:5-6a

PART ONE
PRE-GAME

CHAPTER 1

LET'S NOT THROW IN THE TOWEL: CAUTIOUSLY CELEBRATING THE GIFT OF SPORT

[Upon entering Notre Dame stadium]
This is the most beautiful sight these eyes have ever seen.
— DANIEL RUETTIGER, *Rudy* (1993)

SPORT is one of the many evidences of a gracious God. Allow me to explain. Some of my earliest childhood memories happened on the field of play. Baseball, basketball, tennis, soccer, golf and football – as I write those words, a different memory accompanies each of them. A teammate, a game, an emotion, each is associated with those recreational activities. I'm thankful to God that I was not only blessed to be in those moments but that those moments can be relived in my memories.

One of my fondest memories comes from a particular soccer team (or, football to much of the world) I was part of. It came in the second half, as we possessed a fairly substantial lead over our opponent. As our coach began to substitute players to ensure fatigue would not follow us into the ensuing game, we noticed that our opponent made a notable substitution as well. The player that made his way onto the field caught our attention. Not because of his skill, or his speed, or his stature; but because it was apparent to us that this player had special needs.

As the game moved along, we could tell that this young man's Down's Syndrome made basic skills a challenge for him.

Dribbling a ball, basic coordination, and mental skills were far more laborious for this player. In a real sense, one could easily say that he worked harder than any player on that field, for the challenges he had to overcome to be playing were far greater. The impact this opposing player had on our team was immediate. It was so strong in each of us that we came up with a new objective – *Let him score.*

As the game continued, the ball made its way to this young gentleman at his midfield. As he began to dribble past one defender then another and another, the cheers from his fans began to grow. Before we knew it, he was at our midfield with one more defender to pass. The cheers were louder as he found himself face-to-face with our goalkeeper. As he extended his leg to make the shot, our goalkeeper dove just enough to ensure the ball rolled past his fingertips and into the goal. He jumped up and down, his team was elated and many of our players extended a high-five for his efforts.

Later that week our coach informed us that the coach of the opposing team had contacted him. He thanked him for the kindness our team showed to his player. He said how much it meant to him as a coach but also how much it meant to the team. It turns out that the young boy was so overjoyed he wore his jersey to church the next day.

Of all the teams and all the games I have been a part of, this one remains a memory I cherish. I can remember some excellent wins on our football team. I can remember being the MVP (Most Valuable Player) of a basketball game after making the winning shot (I primarily remember this because I stink at basketball.) I can remember many blessings, but I think it's safe to say they come in second to this one.

You see, that young man lived a challenged life from birth, challenges that only grew with each ensuing year. Most likely, this young man's parents lived a challenged life as well, since the day of his birth when the doctors sat down to have a discussion with them. We can assume his parents noticed the peering eyes of strangers as they walked through supermarkets filled with people who noticed something was different about their son. Perhaps his parents struggled to find a community for this young boy to thrive in. Most likely, this young man's parents were often overcome with thoughts of the future. Will he outlive us? Who will take care of him? Will he have friends? Can he function on his own?

My team's interaction with this boy's life was brief; we didn't even know his name. We were introduced to him as the whistle blew and parted company as we said 'Good game' in our opposing lines at the end of regulation. However, in that brief moment on that obscure field in a small town in Mississippi, this young boy and his parents were, by God's grace, hopefully left with a taste of heaven. And all of it happened through sport.

Life in the Garden

As we open the Word of God, we don't simply read that things were good, we read that they were '*very good*' (Gen. 1:31). God spoke all things into being and placed man and woman in this perfect existence with everything they would need. '… Behold, I have given you every plant yielding seed that is on the face of all the earth, and every tree with seed in its fruit. You shall have them for food' (Gen. 1:29). But the best part of all was that they were face-to-face with their Creator. Unending fellowship without pain or sickness to hinder their happiness with the most gracious Being in all of creation. In short, it was absolute perfection.[1]

Sadly, this existence only lasts two chapters. We are told that a serpent makes his way onto the scene, moving this man and this woman to doubt. You see, God gave and gave and gave to Adam and Eve, but He also set a boundary of protection

---

1. It is important to point out that fallen humans cannot fully fathom the truth just stated. As J. I. Packer states, 'The act of creation is mystery to us; there is more in it than we can understand… To say that [God] created "out of nothing" is to confess the mystery, not explain it'. *Concise Theology: A Guide to Historic Christian Beliefs* (Wheaton, Ill: Tyndale House Publishers, Inc., 1993), p. 21.

around one thing. '...You may surely eat of every tree of the garden' [said God], 'but of the tree of the knowledge of good and evil you shall not eat, for in the day that you eat of it you shall surely die' (Gen. 2:16-17). God gave Adam and Eve all they could ever want, but they were led to focus on the one thing they couldn't have.

The crafty serpent enters into this fruitful seed-bearing garden and plants a new seed, a seed of doubt. '... He said to the woman, "Did God actually say, 'You shall not eat of any tree in the garden'?"' (Gen. 3:1). And this doubt was no small thing; it questioned the goodness of this good Creator who had just made all things very good. Unfortunately, this serpent was also *very good* at selling lies, and the man and woman believed him instead of the One who gave them life. Thus, their doubts about God and their disobedience towards Him brought sin into creation.[2]

Christians believe that the effects of sin cover every square inch of creation – even birth. This is why there are those born with special needs. That young boy from the soccer game displayed many things to us on that field, and one of those things was that we live in a fallen world. His Down's Syndrome illustrated that creation has been marred by sin. His inability to play like his teammates, look like his teammates, or talk like his teammates displayed the effects of Adam and Eve's rebellion in the Garden. However, his life illustrated what lies beneath the surface in each of those present that day.

While every player may have looked normal, played normally, and socially acted normally, each of us was broken. The all-star full of pride who played for his own glory, the quick-tempered fullback who played aggressively from a heart of anger, the insecure athlete who placed too much importance

---

2. '[I]t is to be observed, that punishment was not inflicted upon the first of our race so as to rest on those two alone, but was extended generally to all their posterity, in order that we might know that the human race was cursed in their person.' John Calvin, *Commentaries on the First Book of Moses Called Genesis* (Grand Rapids, MI: Baker Book House, 1979), p. 172.

on his performance, the jealous parent who wished their son was more of a star, the coach who made the game more about himself than his players. It is true that one player appeared more broken than the others, but the hearts of all present that day were – and still are – poisoned with sin.

Yet, in the midst of all the brokenness, something glorious happened. The broken players, the broken parents, and the broken coaches got a glimpse of what life was like prior to Adam and Eve's rebellion. This 'glimpse' of creation, pre-fall, is something theologians often refer to as *common grace.*

We see this notion of common grace in the Sermon on the Mount when Jesus states that God's good blessings are enjoyed by all of humanity, '... For he makes his sun rise on the evil and on the good, and sends rain on the just and on the unjust' (Matt. 5:45b). Common grace are 'those general operations of the Holy Spirit,' says Louis Berkhof, 'whereby He, without renewing the heart, exercises such a moral influence on man that sin is restrained, order is maintained in social life, and civil righteousness is promoted.'[3] That glimpse, as was stated, seemed to 'restrain sin, maintain order, and promote civil righteousness.' All at the field that day, partook of God's common grace through His gift of sport.

True Recreation vs. Current Recreation

I am not the first to point out the significance of the word *recreation.* In light of a discussion on the creation and fall of mankind, the word recreation is interesting. In a very real sense our recreation is *re-creating* what has been broken. Therefore, it is not a stretch to claim that that moment on the soccer field was pointing us back to what life in the Garden must have been like. We were re-creating what was broken. Both teams were

---

3. Louis Berkhof *A Summary of Christian Doctrine* (Carlisle, PA: The Banner of Truth Trust, 1960), p. 111. Berkhof goes on to say that the effects of common grace are made evident in the fact that, 'The natural man is still able to perform natural good or civil righteousness, works that are outwardly in harmony with the law, though without spiritual value.' p. 112.

unified, all players were celebrating, each parent applauded, joy was shared by all; for that one brief moment we forgot about that player's handicap and shared a special unity. Although fleeting, it was a picture of perfection.

The chances are that those of you reading this were not present at this particular soccer game. However, the chances are that each one of you reading this book has experienced moments like this through sports. Even though many of our glorious sports moments are at the expense of our opponents, a team victory displays a unity that points to the perfection that was present in the Garden.

The truth of recreation displaying this common grace is why movies like *Hoosiers, Rudy, Remember the Titans, Cinderella Man, & The Natural* exist. Each of these movies moves us to tears because it touches on this truth.[4] They are giving us a glimpse of what creation looked like prior to the marring of sin. The good guy wins. The underdog defeats the glory-hungry enemy. The team strives together towards a common goal. All of these truths find their origin prior to the entrance of sin. Unfortunately, these movies are just a glimpse, and a glimpse is fading.

While it is very true that our recreation displays this pre-fall existence, it is just as true to say that our current recreation accurately displays the fall of mankind. For Christians to remain faithful when discussing the subject of sports, we must

---

4. 'The origin of the doctrine of common grace was occasioned by the fact that there is in the world, alongside of the course of the Christian life with all its blessings, a natural course of life, which is not redemptive and yet exhibits many traces of the true, the good, and the beautiful.' It is also true that the only reason mankind can even notice common grace is due to more grace. Berkhof later says, 'It is due to common grace that man still retains some sense of the true, the good, and the beautiful.' That is to say, if it were not for this doctrine of common grace, mankind would be so blinded by their sin, they would be unaware of what grace was; therefore, they would be unable to recognize what is true, good and beautiful. Louis Berkhof, *Systematic Theology* (Grand Rapids, MI: William B. Eerdmans Publishing Company, 1932), pp. 432 and 442.

be willing to offer critique of something that can be beautiful at times, yet be so ugly at others. To say it another way, sports can move us to tears of joy, but it can also move us to weep and long for the return of King Jesus.

The countless stories of parents physically assaulting coaches and referees, players that have intentionally injured an opposing player, or the players that have sustained life-altering and life-ending injuries, all point to life in a broken world.[5] Our sports can be so beautiful while also being so brutal. My eyes were opened to this sometime in college as I attended a high school baseball game.

I was working in student ministry and came as a spectator to cheer on one of my students. As I waited for his turn at bat, I sat mouth agape, not from cheering, but from shock. Shock at the mother that berated her son in front of the entire crowd. With every strike her son received, her temper grew. With every strike, her disapproval became apparent. With every strike, the love for her son appeared to wane. As her son finally struck out before the crowd, she screamed: 'Good! I'm glad you struck out! Sit down! You're pathetic.' I was in disbelief.

It was at that moment that my perspective on sports began to shift. I had played sports my entire life. I was a scholarship athlete at a junior college. Needless to say, I loved sports – still do. However, my eyes were gradually opened to the dark side of sports. Rather, should I say, my eyes were opened to the darkness that lies in the heart of mankind and often spills over onto the field. A pastor named Jeremy Treat helped me to see that sports are not the problem, we are.[6] Sports in and of

---

5. The story of Mack Breed, the assistant coach at John Jay High School in San Antonio, instructing his players to 'take out' a referee comes to mind. Breed pled guilty to assault. Julia Jacobo, 'High School Football Coach Who Told Players to "Take Out" Referee Pleads Guilty to Assault,' December 14, 2015, http://abcnews.go.com/Sports/john-jay-assistant-coach-mack-breed-put-18/story?id=35765975; last accessed March 2018.

6. Jeremy Treat, 'More Than a Game: A Theology of Sport,' *Themelios* 40, no. 3 (2015): pp. 398-400.

themselves are not evil, we are (Gen. 3, Rom. 3). It is our sinful hearts that make a good thing, like recreation, something other than honoring to God. As Dr. David Prince says, 'When I was younger, I certainly corrupted the gift of athletics by treating it as an ultimate end rather than an opportunity to worship the God who alone is ultimate.'[7] That night on the ball-field was illustrative of this point.

Keep It Between the Ditches

My grandfather, whom we lovingly referred to as 'Poppy', had some pretty clever sayings. I heard one of these on a particular occasion when he loaned me his car. I am very thankful for the car my parents got me – they didn't even have to provide me with one – but my grandfather's car was much nicer. No, he did not have a sports car, but it was a later model than mine, and it drove much more smoothly. It also didn't possess the quirks mine did. For example, there was a point in time when my car would honk every time you turned the steering wheel to the left – I'm not making this up. I finally removed the fuse from my car because the embarrassment of random honks at strangers was too much for my teenage heart to bear. All of this only fed my desire to drive Poppy's car.

He wasn't the slightest bit reluctant to allow me to drive it at my request, which gives testimony to his kind and gentle heart. I simply asked if I could drive. Without a pause, he said 'Sure.' And as I made my way to the driveway he simply said, 'Keep it between the ditches.' In other words, don't wreck it.

When it comes to a conversation on sports, we need to heed my grandfather's advice – we need to *keep it between the ditches*. That is to say, we need to avoid extremes. Sports are a great gift, but they are not to be worshiped like many of us do. Sports display life in a sinful world, but they are not to be avoided like the plague. We must avoid the extreme of being too anti-sport

---

7. David Prince. *In the Arena: The Promise of Sports for Christian Discipleship* (Nashville, TN: B&H Books, 2016). Kindle edition.

that we miss their beauty, while avoiding the extreme of being so pro-sport that we engage without discernment.

'Sports are a good gift from God, but like all good gifts, sports are corrupted and broken in our fallen world,' says Prince, 'Anyone who thinks that sports automatically cultivate good character simply is not paying attention or purposefully ignoring reality. Sports as ultimate turns a good thing into an idol. Idols are almost always good gifts of God that are treated like God – as the ultimate source of satisfaction.'[8] This is why I say we must *cautiously celebrate the gift of sport*. We must be discerning and cautious of how the human heart can turn good things into ultimate things. That is the aim of this book – to celebrate the good and warn of the bad.

That being said, I would be disingenuous if I didn't say that I fear the church has swerved into the ditch of pro-sport engagement without discernment. I fear many in the church have embraced the love of sport to such a degree that any criticism may fall on deaf ears and simply be dismissed. Dr. Shirl Hoffman, in his book, *Good Game*, addresses this when he says, 'Some thought it brash that I would dare criticize sports at all. It was then that I first realized how reticent the Christian community was to think critically about sports or to explore seriously how the sporting culture intersects with the spiritual path Christians claim to follow.'[9] It is my prayer that you are reading this book because you are attempting to cultivate a heart of discernment towards sports. Whether you are participating in sports or simply a spectator, engage with discernment.

Sports Being Illustrative of a Good God

Earlier I said, 'Sport is one of the many evidences of a gracious God.' Hopefully this chapter has illustrated what a good God

---

8. David Prince, *In the Arena*. Kindle edition.

9. Shirl Hoffman, *Good Game: Christianity and the Culture of Sports* (Waco, TX: Baylor University Press, 2010), p. XIII.

we serve. As we think back to the Garden, we saw a rebellious Adam and Eve still being loved by their gracious Creator. God would have been completely justified to utterly destroy Adam and Eve at the very moment of their sin, but He didn't. Why? Because He is good and gracious. God warned that Adam and Eve would surely die if they ate of the tree (2:17), but He allowed them to endure. The death God promised was not immediate; it was eventual. That, in and of itself, was gracious. If you think back to our discussion of common grace, this too, was God manifesting His grace by allowing mankind to endure. To quote Berkhof once more, 'The execution of the sentence of death on man is deferred. God did not at once fully execute the sentence of death on the sinner, and does not so now, but gives him time for repentance.'[10]

Not only did God not kill them, He also promised that One was going to come to save them. God says, 'I will put enmity between you and the woman, and between your offspring and her offspring; he shall bruise your head and you shall bruise his heel' (Gen. 3:15). These rebellious humans who questioned God's goodness had more goodness poured upon them after their sin. Instead of disowning them, God promised that there would be an 'offspring' to come who would utterly destroy this serpent.

And, if a promised deliverer weren't enough, God continued to give Adam and Eve life. But He does not simply provide them with a life filled with drab colors and bland living. He gives them – and us – steak, pineapple, bacon, coffee, cookies, and shrimp. He gives them – and us – not black, white and grey, but red, orange, yellow, green, blue, indigo, violet, and a thousand other shades of each. He gives them – and us – laughter, joy, and excitement. He does not give them – or us – desert only, but mountains, trees, waterfalls, sun, moon, and stars.

The God of the Old and New Testaments would have been completely just if He had given us nothing; if He left us, if He

---

10. Louis Berkhof, *A Summary of Christian Doctrine.* p. 112.

turned His back on us, if He ended all of creation right then and there. But God, in His head-scratching goodness, gave us more and more ... and more.

God gave us sports. So many fond memories and joy-filled occasions are filled with sports. He did not have to give us anything, He owed us nothing, but He gave us football, golf, basketball, baseball, soccer, volleyball, swimming, tennis and much, much more. Grace gives you what you don't deserve. In many ways grace doesn't make sense. And, sports illustrate the fact that God is gracious.

Sports are a gracious gift from God, but, just like any gift, it must be stewarded in order to be properly appreciated. The purpose of this book is to assist Christians in their enjoyment of God's good gift of sports. In order for Christians to enjoy the good gift of sports, they must exercise the biblical concept of stewardship; a concept we'll unpack more later. Therefore, this book will look at stewardship in six specific ways: stewardship of our identities, time, bodies, money, worship, and the souls of our children.

Since fallen human begins are prone to misuse God's good gifts, we must be calling on the Holy Spirit while we seek to steward the gifts He bestows. If not, the good gifts of God will become what all of His misused gifts become: idols. This is what we will discuss in the next chapter.

CHAPTER 2

IS OUR PLAY GODLY OR GODLESS?

Uh, Lord, hallowed be Thy name. May our feet be swift; may our bats be mighty ... God, these are good girls, and they work hard. Just help them see it all the way through. Okay, that's it.

— JIMMY DUGAN, *A League of Their Own* (1992)

FOR many, Tom Brady is considered to be one of the greatest quarterbacks to ever play the game of football. He is equally loved and loathed by any who follow the National Football League. Whether or not you are a lover or hater of Brady, his name will inevitably find its way into a discussion on elite quarterbacks.

A few years ago, he was interviewed on the television show *60 Minutes*. As he was reflecting on his years in the game, his many accomplishments, and the millions he was making from football, he said something that should resonate with anyone who has a heartbeat. At the time of this interview he had won three Super Bowls (he has now won four), and he said, 'Why do I have three Super Bowl rings and still think there's something greater out there for me? There's gotta be more than this.' In essence Brady was saying, 'I've accomplished all you can hope to accomplish in the NFL, and it still isn't enough.'

Now, whether you are a Christian or not, this statement should rock you to your core. Here is a person who has reached a level in life many will never reach. Young men grow up longing, dreaming, striving to get where Brady is. They hope to be that Super Bowl quarterback or receiver or running back and have structured much of their life around this specific longing. Yet here is a guy who has been on the other side telling us it isn't enough. It will not bring fulfillment. It cannot.

Unbelievers hear this statement and think, 'This guy has won the greatest game you can play in football, multiple times. He has a supermodel wife. He has more money than I will ever see. And there's something that's leaving him unsatisfied.'

Believers hear this statement and think, 'This guy has won the greatest game you can play in football, multiple times. He has a supermodel wife. He has more money than I will ever see. And there's something that's leaving him unsatisfied.'

Believers know Brady needs Christ. They know about this 'God-shaped-void' in the human heart. They know that Jesus Christ is the only one who can fill that void. They know the answer, yet their struggle is the same as the unbeliever. The fallen human heart just doesn't believe that God can bring ultimate satisfaction, so it looks for it elsewhere resulting in idolatry. G. K. Beale defines idolatry as, 'whatever your heart clings to or relies on for ultimate security.'[1]

Stewardship recognizes a Creator and all things flowing from that Creator, as stated in chapter one. Therefore, idolatry, is the polar opposite of stewardship. It's perverting gifts that were meant to glorify the Giver.[2] '[T]he primal problem with idolatry,' says Beale, 'is that it blurs the distinction between the Creator God and the creation. This both damages creation (including ourselves) and diminishes the glory of the Creator.'[3]

God's Top Ten

Not too long ago I was taking my son, Samuel, camping. It was the first time the two of us were going – just the men! As we were

---

1. Beale modifies this definition from Martin Luther's, 'whatever your heart clings to and relies upon, that is your God; truth and faith of the heart alone make both God and idol.' G. K. Beale *We Become What We Worship: A Biblical Theology of Worship* (Downers Grove, Ill: IVP Academic, 2008), Kindle edition.

2. David Prince uses the language of weaponry when abusing God's good gifts when he says, '[S]ometimes sports become an idolatrous weapon wielded against God.' *In the Arena*. Kindle edition.

3. G. K. Beale. *We Become What We Worship*. Kindle edition.

driving down the road, I told Samuel to think of some questions to ask me about the Bible. I told him to be thinking, and I assumed it might be several minutes before something came to mind. However, in less than a minute, he was ready with a question.

To be honest, I was assuming it would be a 'softball' question – Why is the sky blue? Why do giraffes have long necks? – something along those lines. But my son took me in an entirely different direction. 'Dad,' he said, 'Why did God give us the Ten Commandments?' For a split-second, I contemplated turning on the radio and just avoiding the conversation. It caught me off guard and, after all, it was an insightful question so I didn't want to answer unwisely. My knee-jerk answer, however, was this: 'Because God loves us. He gave us the Ten Commandments, Son, because He loves us.'

I think my response was somewhat shaped by the misconceptions most have when thinking about the Ten Commandments. Many in our day see them as rigid and restrictive boundaries set up by a fun-sucking, kill-joy god. Calvin says that our misunderstanding of God ultimately lies in the 'shroud of darkness' all of mankind is covered in.[4] In all likelihood, many Christians in the church probably think about the Ten Commandments in this way as well. But they are given to us because God loves us. They are given for God's ultimate glory and our good. You see, God knew mankind far better than we do, and He knew we would kill ourselves and harm others if He did not place these loving boundaries around our fallen hearts.

Before God gives the Ten Commandments in Exodus 20, He reminds us of something crucial to our understanding. We

---

4. '[M]an is so shrouded in the darkness of errors that he hardly begins to grasp through this natural law what worship is acceptable to God. Surely he is very far removed from a true estimate of it. Besides this, he is so puffed up with haughtiness and ambition, and so blinded by self-love, that he is as yet unable to look upon himself and, as it were, to descend within himself, that he may humble and abase himself and confess his own miserable condition.' John Calvin. *The Institutes of the Christian Religion.* (Louisville, KY: Westminster John Knox Press, 1929), p. 368.

read, 'I am the LORD your God, who brought you out of the land of Egypt, out of the house of slavery' (Exod. 20:2). These verses not only remind us that God claims us as His people and we get to claim Him as our God, but we are also reminded of a very important order. That is, God has *already* delivered His people when He gives them these commandments.

I am not the first person to point this out, but it is vital in our understanding of all of God's Word.[5] God did not say, 'If you obey all these commandments, I will consider delivering you.' God essentially said, 'I have already delivered you, because you are my children and I love you. Now, out of your love for me and gratitude for what I've done, live a life of obedience.' This changes everything. We do not obey to earn favor from God. We obey because we are favored by God.

Yet, what we need to see, as fallen human beings, is that we will fail[6]. We will sin. We break God's commandments ... daily. And, as we get to Exodus 20:3, 'You shall have no other gods before me,' we must understand what this implies. God's commanding us to have no other gods implies that we will be tempted to have other gods. Again, He's lovingly giving us this command to reveal our false gods so that we will repent of them and run back to Him. We cannot miss the grace here. Yet, we are still fallen and we will attempt to place other things before God.

What Is Worship?

We have many traditions in our family, and one of those consistent traditions is Friday night movie nights. On one particular movie night, we were watching *Monsters University*. (If you haven't seen the movie, this is no major spoiler.) Towards

---

5. Tim Keller. Sermon: *Getting Out*. 2011 TGC National Conference (Plenary Session) Exodus 14. https://www.thegospelcoalition.org/conference_media/gettingout/; last accessed February 2018.

6. '[B]y comparing the righteousness of the law with our life, we learn how far we are from conforming to God's will.' Calvin, *The Institutes of the Christian Religion*, p. 369.

the end of the film, the two remaining scare teams are having a final competition before the entire college campus.

As the scene is set up, it depicts something pretty universal at any college campus. The film shows many monsters congregating toward an arena and each of them singing some sort of university-sounding song. It is a song the entire student body knows and they sing it with great reverence. The manner in which the scene was depicted simply reminded me of many college football games I have attended, and it is obvious that is what the filmmakers were trying to convey.

However, my oldest daughter, Sarah, asked an extremely insightful question. She said, 'Daddy, are they going to church?' As soon as she asked the question, the familiarity with which I was viewing that scene changed. My eyes easily saw the reverence she associated with church. I realized that she was exactly right.

Of course they were not going to church, but they were going to worship.

One of my seminary professors would often say, 'All of life is worship.' Far too often Christians think of worship as a building or something we simply do on Sundays. However, we must see that we are always worshiping someone or something. If Exodus 20:3 tells us anything, it is that we are worshipers. We will either worship the one true God of the Bible, or we will worship a false god. But we will worship. As Ralph Waldo Emerson says, 'A person will worship something, have no doubt about that … That which dominates our imaginations and our thoughts will determine our lives, and our character. Therefore, it behooves us to be careful what we worship, for what we are worshipping we are becoming.'[7] G. K. Beale makes this sobering conclusion: 'The principle is this: if we worship idols, we will become like the idols, and that likeness will ruin us.'[8]

---

7. Ralph Waldo Emerson, adapted by Chaim Stern, *Gates of Understanding*, vol. 1 (New York: Central Conference of American Rabbis, 1977), p. 216.

8. G. K. Beale, *We Become What We Worship*. Kindle edition.

What Tim Keller points out in his book, *Counterfeit Gods*, is that idols are often good things. 'The greater the good,' says Keller, 'the more likely we are to expect that it can satisfy our deepest needs and hopes. Anything can serve as a counterfeit god, especially the very best things in life.'[9] This should not surprise Christians.

For example, consider the way that Satan works. When we first meet him in the Garden of Eden, he doesn't claim that he's opposed to God, rather he quotes God ... or misquotes him, I should say.[10] He comes to Eve quoting the One she is aligned with, quoting her Creator. Satan doesn't come out and exclaim that he hates God and he's his enemy, he uses the very words of God against Eve. The important thing to note is his craftiness. He is subtle.

The same is true of our idols. Rarely are our idols exceedingly wicked things we enjoy doing. Don't get me wrong; they are wicked from the standpoint of worshiping them over God, but they are rarely inherently wicked. I would say the following are some of the more popular idols of our culture and none of them are wicked in their essence: family, friends, money, and sex.

Now, I understand that many will stand up and protest the last one – sex. However, let us be reminded that God created sex, called it a good thing, and commands His people to have sex. Sex is not a bad thing; sinful human beings have made it a bad thing. That being said, this culture absolutely worships sex. It's on television, movies, music, magazines, every platform of social media, and, obviously, the Internet.

The important truth to note is that none of those things listed above is evil in and of itself. Family is an amazing institution God established. Friendships are among the greatest blessings God lavishes upon His people. Money is used to put food on

9. Tim Keller, *Counterfeit Gods: The Empty Promises of Money, Sex, and Power, and the Only Hope that Matters* (New York: Dutton, 2009), p. xvii.

10. Russell Moore sparked this thought from an article entitled, 'The Spiritual Warfare of Boring Preaching,' August 10, 2016, http://www.russellmoore.com/2016/08/10/spiritual-warfare-boring-preaching/; last accessed February 2018.

the table, and, if God blesses you with a lot of it, you can end up blessing many people with your stewardship of it.[11]

Yet each of these becomes wicked when it gets in the hands of sinful people. Family becomes an idol when it becomes a priority over anyone and anything. Friends become an idol if we feel the need to always be around them. Money becomes an idol when we love it too much. And sex becomes a selfish idol when we view it as the ultimate thing.

I did, however, leave out one of the biggest idols of our culture and the theme of this book: sports.

God vs. Sports

As Christians, there are two dangers when it comes to talking about sports and worship. Both of those dangers are in the extremes I warned about in chapter one, when Poppy said, 'keep it between the ditches'.

On the one extreme, there are Christians who are sinfully worshiping sports. Sports have become an idol in their lives. They wake up checking blogs about their favorite sports teams. They rarely attend church, preferring instead to attend sporting events. The majority of their calendar revolves around the team. If sports is ever spoken of negatively they get angry, unable to accept any criticism in reference to sports. In families, their time and money is devoted way too much to little Johnny's baseball team, theater club, or football league – or, Sally's ballet, basketball, or softball team.

In Mark Jones' article, *Organized Sports on Sundays?* he shares this interchange: 'I recently spoke with a mother of one of my son's teammates. She used to go to church, but, in her words, she said that her children all now have sports on Sundays so they aren't able to go to church anymore.'[12]

---

11. See my article, *Money CAN Buy Happiness*, at www.rym.org; last accessed March 2018.

12. Mark Jones, *Organized Sports on Sundays?* Reformation 21, June 12, 2015, http://www.reformation21.org/blog/2015/06/sports-on-sundays.php; last accessed February 2018.

Kenda Creasy Dean's research in *Almost Christian* seems to point to this as well when she concluded that, 'Religion doesn't claim teenagers' time or attention, compared to other social institutions, activities and organizations.'[13] Dean goes on to say, 'A number of institutions are so built into adolescent's lives – school, the media, peer groups – that teenagers don't even think of them as holding sway over their schedules or decisions. They simply *are*, and teenagers participate in them because they are insidious and pervasive. Teenagers typically view religion, on the other hand, as optional … [R]eligious functions as an "add-on," an extracurricular activity, something you do if you feel like it or if you have time.'[14]

In reference to family sport's idolatry, Ted Kluck says, 'We see [family idolatry] every time we go to a ball game or performing arts event that our kids are involved in. We see it every time we spot a fifth grader's name and number emblazoned on the back of his mother's sweatshirt in the stands of a peewee football game. We see it in every harried family taking different cars in different directions to different sports practices only to reconnect at the end of the night to collapse into bed. We see it in our own hearts when we're disappointed that *our* child may not be the star.'[15]

In their book, *The Faithful Parent,* Martha Peace and Stuart Scott say, 'The teen years are typically filled with activities. There are school and sports and parties and movies and video games, and part-time jobs for some. It often seems that every minute of every day is taken up with something other than the Lord.'[16]

---

13. Kenda Creasy Dean, *Almost Christian: What the Faith of Our Teenagers is Telling the American Church* (New York, New York: Oxford University Press, 2010), p. 205.

14. Ibid. p. 205. Kenda Creasy Dean states that, 'Three out of four American teenagers claim to be Christians, and most are affiliated with a religious organization – but only about half consider it very important, and fewer than half actually practice their faith as a regular part of their lives.'

15. Ted Kluck, *Household Gods: Freed from the Worship of Family to Delight in the Glory of God.* (Colorado Springs, CO: NavPress, 2014), p. 14.

16. Martha Peace and Stuart W. Scott, *The Faithful Parent: A Biblical Guide to Raising a Family.* (Phillipsburg, New Jersey: P&R Publishing, 2010), p. 106.

While there are families neck-deep in sport's idolatry, there is also another extreme. There are Christians who think sports and God are at odds with each other. From the above examples, we can see how sports can be at odds with God and we can turn them into a false god. However, God can truly be honored through (or in) sports, which takes us back to the idea of common grace.

David Prince touches on this notion when relaying his love for baseball. He says, '[W]hen I witness the smooth beauty of a double play, I sense a pale reflection of the beauty and glory of God ... we are capable of reflecting the truth, beauty, and goodness of our Creator God.'[17] If Christians abstain from sports altogether, they will miss out on the grace communicated through sports. To say it another way, God can be worshiped through sports, so Christians must be cautious of over-reacting in their critique of sports.

Let me get at this truth by asking a question. Think of your favorite athlete in your favorite sport. (I know if I mention a specific athlete here, I will be hated by some, so think of your favorite). Here's the question: who gave them their talent? It's the easy, Sunday school answer: God.

God gave that quarterback the arm to throw a dart into the end zone. God gave the legs to the soccer/football player that curves the ball into the upper-right corner of the goal. God gave the arm to the pitcher that can scream a ninety mph fastball over the plate. God gave the Olympians every muscle fiber that moves them to become the best *in the world*. The caution for the Christian lies in our worship of the *creation* over the *Creator*.

Paul warns us of this in Romans 1:18-32. He explains that God reveals Himself to us through creation; this is often referred to as *general revelation*. J. I. Packer says, 'God's world is not a shield hiding the Creator's power and majesty. From the natural order it is evident that a mighty and majestic Creator is

---

17. David Prince, *In the Arena*. Kindle edition.

there.'[18] That is, God speaks to us through creation in the sense that we understand that there is a God through the glorious mountain peak or the vast ocean. Creation tells us God exists when we hold the newborn infant in our arms and see the tiny fingers, toes, and hear the heartbeat, realizing there must be a God who created this tiny life. And creation tells us there's a God when we see an athlete that stands out above the rest and are amazed by their gift.

Athletes and amazing athleticism are forms of general revelation. When we are amazed at a catch in the end zone, or the speed of an individual, or the three-point shot, we are ultimately worshiping *something*, whether we realize it or not. The caution Paul gives comes in verse 25 of Romans 1, '… they exchanged the truth about God for a lie and worshiped and served the creature rather than the Creator, who is blessed forever! Amen.'

Godly Sports

The earlier subheading 'God vs. Sports' was a bit of a trick. Of course, this is often how Christians think of sports, and most of the time Christians critique sports, this is simply what people hear. However, what this chapter clearly illustrates is that sports can display the existence of God. To say it in a way Paul might say it: we can worship the Creator *through* the creation.

The caution for each of us is to fully understand the condition of our heart. Since we are sinful, we will be prone to worship sports. Our sinful hearts will, far too often, worship the creature over the Creator. We must humbly realize that we spend too much time, money, and energy on our children's sports teams, quite often.

Kluck addresses this caution when he says, 'As a coach I've had film sessions and games on Sundays. And even on those

---

18. J. I. Packer, *Concise Theology: A Guide to Historic Christian Beliefs* (Wheaton, Ill: Tyndale House Publishers, Inc., 1993), p. 9. Packer goes on to say, 'General revelation is so called because everyone receives it, just by virtue of being alive in God's world … God's universal revelation of his power, praiseworthiness, and moral claim is the basis of Paul's indictment of the whole human race as sinful and guilty before God for failing to serve him as we should' (Rom. 1:18-3:19).

Sundays when I went to church *before* the game, I confess I wasn't worshipping. I was wondering what to call on third-and-long. I know how difficult this issue is – and it's difficult because of how much I *love* football … The problem comes when I *need* [competition] in order to feel happy or peaceful.'[19] When our sports become a need and a love, we must be cautious of the idolatrous nature of our human heart.

To quote Prince once more, 'I am an unabashed fan of sports, but I do not write this chapter primarily as a fan; rather, I write as a Christian pastor and seminary professor. This discussion of sports fandom begs the question: Is the fanaticism good or bad? My answer is an unequivocal "Yes!" – it all depends on whether sports are summed up in Christ or abstracted from him.'[20]

In order to make our sports a more godly experience and disciple our children in this understanding, we must see the Creator behind the creation. When you cheer an amazing athletic accomplishment, remember the God that is behind that moment, not simply the particular athleticism you just witnessed, but also the emotions that accompany it. The unity that was shared in the stands. The joy that comes out in an eruption of applause. The discussions that take place long after, in some cases years after, the moment is over.

All of it points to our gracious and loving Creator. Christian, do not miss this truth of the great God we worship. By knowing Him and worshiping Him more fully, we will begin to worship sports less and enjoy them on a deeper level. I love how Jeremy Treat says it, '[W]hen viewed through the lens of Scripture, sports are more than game, less than a god, and when transformed by the gospel can be received as a gift to be enjoyed forever.'[21] This greater appreciation can be fostered by our stewardship of sports. The topic of stewardship is something we will discuss in the remainder of this book.

---

19. Kluck Ibid., p. 60.

20. Prince, Ibid, Kindle edition.

21. Jeremy Treat, 'More Than a Game: A Theology of Sport,' *Themelios* 40, no. 3 (2015).

CHAPTER 3

EXERCISING DOMINION ON THE FIELD: STEWARDSHIP OF SPORTS

Great moments ... are born from great opportunity. And that's what you have here, tonight, boys. That's what you've earned here tonight. One game. If we played 'em ten times, they might win nine. But not this game. Not tonight. Tonight, we skate with them. Tonight, we stay with them. And we shut them down because we can! Tonight, WE are the greatest hockey team in the world. You were born to be hockey players. Every one of you. And you were meant to be here tonight. This is your time. Their time is done. It's over. I'm sick and tired of hearing about what a great hockey team the Soviets have. .... This is your time. Now go out there and take it.

— Herb Brooks, *Miracle* (2004)

AS I write this, the 2016 Rio Olympics are taking place. It is such an electric two weeks. A moment where much of the world's attention is focused on one thing: competition. Even though we often cheer for our country over another, it often seems more unifying than divisive. While there is a definite expectation to have our country defeat another, there is also an appreciation for the level of athleticism witnessed, regardless of its point of origin. For example, when we see a human being at the peak of physical fitness perform at a level that exceeds the rest of humanity – across the globe – it's close to impossible for us to lack appreciation for what we just witnessed.

As I was watching a particular event one night, a thought occurred to me. To be completely honest with you, I was noticing the body of one of the competitors. My thoughts were this, *I wonder what sort of discipline that person must employ to maintain a physique like that.* In the midst of that reflective thought, I laughed because of my orange-crusted fingertips, as a bag of Cheetos lay open in my lap. *I'm sure that Olympian doesn't eat Cheetos,* was my accompanying thought!

Regardless of the religious beliefs of any Olympian, or any athlete for that matter, they all embrace a deeply theological truth: *stewardship.* Stewardship is a word that becomes less familiar as you leave Christian circles. It is, no doubt, a biblical word, and because of that it is probably less familiar in everyday life. Joe Carter defines stewardship in this way, '[It] is the wise use of every resource entrusted to us by God – whether money, skill, time, talent or position – for his purposes.'[1]

A steward is someone who is entrusted with the responsibility to care for something. A steward is under the authority of another. '[S]tewardship requires a fundamental commitment to present ourselves completely to God as his servants, with no reservations,' says Hugh Welchel, '[It] is not one more thing we have to do, but a way of seeing everything we already do in a very different light.'[2] A steward is only a steward when they have remained faithful to what is placed under their care.

To use an example from the Olympian I noticed, they were stewarding their body very well. I'm sure they ate a certain number of calories each day. Did a certain amount of reps for their workout routine. Got a certain amount of sleep and stretched their muscles before and after. All of this was a part of stewardship.

Even though these Olympians are the elites when it comes to stewardship of the body, I think most of them wouldn't call what they are doing stewardship. Why would I say that? Because of what stewardship implies. You see, stewardship implies *ownership.*

---

1. Joe Carter, *NIV Lifehacks Bible: Practical Tools for Successful Spiritual Habits* (Grand Rapids, MI: Zondervan, 2015), p. 51.

2. Hugh Welchel, 'David's Mighty Men: Stewardship in Action,' *Institute for Faith, Work, and Economics,* www.blog.tifwe.org/davids-mighty-men-stewardship-in-action/; last accessed February 2018.

'... [T]here is not a square inch in the whole domain of human existence over which Christ, who is sovereign over all, does not cry: Mine!'[3] In light of this, Joe Carter says, 'We rob God when we take for ourselves what belongs to him ... We rob God when we try to carve out a space – whether in our thoughts, our time or our finances and try to say, "This belongs to me".'[4]

Who's the Boss?

Paul David Tripp once said that the four most significant words in all of human history were, 'In the beginning, God ...' (Gen. 1:1a). '[W]ith those four words,' Tripp says, 'everything in life is given its shape, purpose, and meaning.'[5] Before anything existed, God was, simply and profoundly, there. Let's think about that a bit more intently.

God predates fire and water. He predates grass, plants, and trees. Before lions, tigers, bears, dolphins, sharks, clown fish, shrimp and plankton, God was there. He was before solar systems, stars, the moon, and the sun. Before the wheel, wagons, cars, boats, airplanes, telephones, skyscrapers, computers, iPods, iPhones, Apple, or Microsoft were a concept in the human mind, God was there. Before movies, Alfred Hitchcock, Stephen Spielberg, Clark Gabel, Ingrid Bergman, Grace Kelly, James Stewart, Tom Hanks, or Meryl Streep ever mouthed a single syllable, God was there. Even before gender, sex, marriage, family or the church were created, God existed. Long before Bo Jackson, Michael Jordan, Joe Montana, Aaron Rodgers, Mia Hamm, Tiger Woods, Serena Williams, and Michael Phelps took a step, stroke, swing, or tossed a ball, God was there. Centuries and centuries before George Washington, Abraham Lincoln, John F. Kennedy, Ronald Reagan or Barak Obama constructed their

---

3. Abraham Kuyper, *Abraham Kuyper: A Centennial Reader* (Grand Rapids, MI: William B. Eerdmans, 1998), p. 121.

4. Joe Carter, *NIV Lifehacks Bible*, p. 1142.

5. Paul David Tripp, *Sex & Money: Pleasures that Leave You Empty and Grace that Satisfies* (Wheaton, IL: Crossway, 2013), p. 27.

first sentence, God spoke. While Winston Churchill, Napoleon, Julius Caesar, Adolph Hitler, George S. Patton, & Gandhi were still crawling in diapers, God was ruling.

These four words tell us God was and is much more significant than you or I ever will be. It is in these four words that all of life finds its meaning. In short, these four words tell us who the boss is. Since God thought up the intricacies of the human heart, we should thank Him for every beat. Since God knows every firing of every synapse, it would be a good idea to use the brain He gave us for His glory. Since God placed every muscle fiber, tendon, and ligament in place, it should be expected that human beings should care for them. Since God invented life, we take our cues from Him.

David tells us, 'The earth is the Lord's, and everything in it, the world, and all who live in it; for he founded it on the seas and established it on the waters' (Ps. 24:1-2, NIV). It is this core truth that led Lester DeKoster and Gerard Berghoef to say, 'Stewardship is far more than the handling of our money. Stewardship is the handling of life, and time, and destiny.'[6]

God is the one who gets to tell mankind what to do. Not kings, presidents, rulers, athletes, celebrities, warriors, terrorists, pastors, feminists, male chauvinists, racists, Republicans, Democrats, or Independents, not only because God is God, but also because these will soon return to dust and God's glory will never, ever fade! He is the Creator of all that ever has been, all that is, and all that will be.

Ultimately, God deserves all the glory for any earthly accomplishment. When we take credit for what we have, we are attempting to rob God of the grace He's bestowed upon us.[7]

6. Lester DeKoster and Gerard Berghoef, *Faithful in All God's House* (Christian's Library Press, 2013) Quoted in *NIV Lifehacks Bible*.

7. This thought originated with 'How to Not Rob God' section in Joe Carter's *NIV Lifehacks Bible*. Carter says, 'Recognize that God deserves all the credit – A second way we rob God is to steal the credit for what we have', p. 1142.

There is a sense in which everything that has ever been invented, is being invented, and will be invented has His patent on it. Every book that has ever been written has His authorship stamped on the cover. Every gold medal, silver medal, and bronze medal belongs to Him, as well as everyone who ever makes it to the Olympics, as well as everyone who has taken one athletic step in their life has taken it because He allowed it. He enables the talents of the participants in every Super Bowl, every Stanley Cup, every Masters, every National Championship in every sport, ever.

Every good accomplishment is His. He deserves the applause, He deserves the podium, He deserves the platform, He deserves the parade, He deserves the keys to the city, He deserves to have His jersey worn, He's the one who should have arenas filled cheering His name, because He's the Owner of all that has been, all that is, and all that will be. This is the God of every living and inanimate object.

In the Beginning, God …

This all-powerful God gives humanity their first instructions. In Genesis 1:28, we receive this command: 'And God blessed [Adam and Eve]. And God said to them, "Be fruitful and multiply and fill the earth and subdue it, and have *dominion* over the fish of the sea and over the birds of the heavens and over every living thing that moves on the earth".' (Emphasis mine)

Since God is the boss, we know that He comes first. Now, the Boss graciously gives us a further knowledge of the 'pecking order,' or food chain, if you will. God tells mankind they have dominion over creation. They are over the plant and animal kingdoms. They are more beautiful and glorious than the rest of creation, because we are told, prior to verse 28, that mankind was created after the likeness of this eternal God (Gen. 1:27).

Oftentimes theologians refer to this exercise of dominion as the *creation mandate*. Essentially, the creation mandate is God's commanding mankind to take care of creation. God works to bring about creation, but He commands mankind to carry on this work.[8] Albert Wolters provides a helpful illustration in his book, *Creation Regained*, when he says:

> *The creation mandate provides a sort of climax to the six days of creation. The stage with all its rich variety of props has been set by the stage director, the actors are introduced, and as the curtain rises and the stage director moves backstage, they are given their opening cue. The drama of human history is about to begin, and the first and foundational Word of God to his children is the command to 'fill and subdue'.*[9]

Not only does this include the tilling of the ground or man's authority and care over the animal kingdom, mankind is to care for their own bodies as well. However, 'In the beginning, God …' tells us our bodies are not ours … but God's.

This is where the idea of ownership becomes so significant and where Christians and non-Christians may deviate in their thinking. For the unbeliever, the toil in exercise is often to simply be the greatest. To win the prize. To be the one at the top of the platform. To represent their country.

In addition, there are negative factors creeping into their motives. They could simply strive to be the greatest from a sense of pride and arrogance. They could sculpt their physique from a heart of vanity. Their drive may find its source in jealousy over the accomplishments and accolades of another.

However, the heart of the believer is not immune to these same sins. Pride, arrogance, vanity, and jealousy know no bounds when it comes to the human heart. The Christian heart is not free from these temptations. Yes, the Christian heart is freed from being held captive by these sins, but it is still enticed by them.

---

8. Tim Keller, *Every Good Endeavor: Connecting Your Work to God's Work* (New York, New York: Riverhead Books, 2012), p. 22. Keller says, '[T]hough all God had made was good, it was still to a great degree undeveloped. God left creation with deep untapped potential for cultivation that people were to unlock through their labor.'

9. Albert Wolters, *Creation Regained: Biblical Basics for a Reformational Worldview* (Grand Rapids, MI: William B. Eerdmans Publishing Company), p. 43.

As I've heard it said before, when Christ comes into our hearts, the *power* of sin has been broken, but the *presence* of sin remains. The sin that is present in the heart of any athlete is something Christians must be aware of in their pursuit of sports.[10]

Exercising Dominion

There was a brief time in college when I began to play racquetball. The gym on our college campus had several racquetball courts. At first, they were merely something I would pay a passing glance to on my way to the gym. After a while, my curiosity got the better of me, and I ventured onto one of the courts with my friends. Without knowing the rules, or much technique for that matter, my friend and I simply began to hit the ball … really hard.

After a few months, I began to play better and become a bit more competitive. Full disclosure, I was never a phenomenal athlete, but I had some athleticism that I was able to utilize in this sport. All of this to say, I would typically beat the friends I played.

One day, as I was waiting for my friend to meet me at the gym, an older man asked me if I wanted to play racquetball. I informed him that I was waiting for a friend. To which he replied, with a hint of indignation, I might add, 'He's not here, is he?' So I said, 'Okay. Let's play.' But, internally I was thinking, 'Get ready old man. I'm about to destroy you.'

What began as my polite attempt to take it easy on this 'old man,' ended with me out of breath having only scored two points on him. I was amazed at how precisely this man could hit the ball. He had me running all over the court, and he seemed

---

10. Tim Keller discusses this when referencing work, but it definitely carries over to athletics. 'One of the reasons work is both fruitless and pointless is the powerful inclination of the human heart to make work, and its attendant benefits, the main basis of one's meaning and identity. When this happens, work is no longer a way to create and bring out the wonders of the created order, as Calvin would say, or to be an instrument of God's providence, serving the basic needs of our neighbor, as Luther would say.' Tim Keller, *Every Good Endeavor*, p. 108.

to hardly break a sweat. After he mopped the floor with me in our first game, I was a bit more prepared with the second one. I wasn't going to hold back. I would start more aggressively, I thought. The fact that I scored a grand total of five points on him in our second match really taught him a lesson, I'm sure. He utterly dominated me. A man twice my age not only gave me a lesson in humility that day, but in stewardship as well.

Dominion means to exercise power or control. It can be another word for sovereign. Perhaps notions of kings ruling may come to mind. When I say that the older man *dominated* me on the racquetball court, I'm saying he was in control. Ruling my every move. Displaying a power over me. This is what athletes mean when they speak of a greater opponent dominating them.

Likewise, God exercises His sovereign control and power over all creation. However, in His grace, He imparts authority to mankind by giving us dominion over creation. Not only is mankind set apart because of being God's image-bearers, we are also set apart by this responsibility of dominion which God imparts. And, our dominion over creation is demonstrated in our stewardship of it, not our abuse of it. To quote Keller again, 'God owns the world, but he has put it under our care to cultivate it. It is definitely not a mandate to treat the world and its resources as if they are ours to use, exploit, and discard as we wish … [T]he word 'subdue' indicates that even in its original, unfallen form, God made the world to need work.'[11]

In light of this, our stewardship responsibility is far vaster than the stewardship of our bodies in athletics. 'At its most basic level, biblical stewardship is holistic and missional, touching every area of life and employing every legitimate vocation in service to Jesus Christ.'[12] It is no doubt true that Christians are

---

11. Tim Keller, *Every Good Endeavor*, pp. 45-46.

12. Stephen Grabill, *The Church's Call to Steward God's Mission in the World*, The Gospel Coalition, August 19, 2014. https://www.thegospelcoalition.org/article/the-churchs-call-to-steward-gods-mission-in-the-world; last accessed February 2018.

to steward the bodies God graciously gives, but Christians are to steward much more.

For example, every dime we own belongs to God. Every second of every day is God's, not ours. When Christians truly believe that God is the owner of all things, it affects the way we live our lives. When we realize our money isn't ours, but was graciously given to us by God, we spend it differently. When we realize our time belongs to God, we invest it discerningly. When we realize our very bodies belong to the Lord, it impacts what we put into them and how we care for them.

To Whom Do You Belong?

There is an excellent book entitled, *Thoughts to Make Your Heart Sing*, by Sally-Lloyd Jones. I'm hesitant to call it a children's book, because it is excellent for adults as well, but it's written for children and has pictures (sorry there aren't any pictures in this book). One of our family's favorite stories in the book is about a young, black girl who is sold in a slave auction. The following paraphrase will illustrate my point:

As the little girl is sold as property to this new 'master,' he turns to her and says, 'You're free.' This, of course, is strange to this young girl because she's never known freedom. As the man informs her of her freedom, she inquires further, 'Free to go anywhere? Free to do anything?' Because this sense of freedom breaks any category she has. It is absolutely foreign to her. The man laughingly says, 'Absolutely. You're free to do whatever you want and go wherever you want to go.' The young girl replies: 'Then I will go with you ... I will go with you.'[13]

You see, this girl may have lived a horrific life of enslavement. She may have been sold and resold to countless individuals at a young age. As she is sold again, she is given something she's never had: freedom. Yet, instead of running off and living apart from this new 'master,' she wanted to remain by his side.

---

13. Sally Lloyd-Jones, *Thoughts to Make Your Heart Sing* (Grand Rapids: Zonderkids, 2012), pp. 118-19.

Although this master now 'owned' her, this ownership was not burdensome. Therefore, she wanted to go where he went and do what he did.

What about you? To whom do you belong? If you belong to Jesus Christ, you are His. While the apostle Paul is dealing with sexual sin among God's people, he makes this statement: 'You are not your own, for you were bought with a price' (1 Cor. 6:19b-20a). If you claim the name of Jesus, He has bought you with His blood. With His atoning sacrifice on the cross, He had you in mind.

It is out of this knowledge that our stewardship should flow. If Jesus has purchased us with His blood, our time, our bodies, our money is His, not ours. Yet, when we understand what He gave for us, it should allow us to give our time, bodies, and money away for Him. Christians do not do this to earn favor with God; rather, we do it out of thanksgiving for what Jesus Christ did for us.

This idea of stewardship will be the foundation for the remainder of this book. With the understanding of God's almighty power, authority, and ownership in place, and the authority He grants us as stewards, how are we to engage in the sphere of sports? How can we best steward the resources He's given us to give Him maximum glory? These questions will be in focus as we move forward.

PART TWO
GAME TIME

CHAPTER 4

PERFORMANCE-BASED RELIGION: STEWARDSHIP OF IDENTITY

I will not rest until I have you holding a Coke, wearing your own shoe, playing a Sega game featuring you, while singing your own song in a commercial starring you, broadcast during the Super Bowl, in a game that you are winning, and I will not sleep until that happens.

— JERRY MAGUIRE, *Jerry Maguire* (1996)

SOCCER has been a major part of my life. My passion to play soccer was very strong when I was young. I loved to play soccer, but I didn't have a lot of natural athleticism. Since I'm average when it comes to athleticism, much of my ability came from years of practice and work. Therefore, I invested years in the sport of soccer. I participated in countless practices, traveled to countless tournaments, and played in countless games. Basically, since five-year-old kindergarten into college I played soccer. I played in junior college and then played in a club league at a university.

I remember when soccer began to come to an end in my life. I can vividly remember my last high school game. I remember it was foggy that night, and I remember we lost. I remember, towards the end of the game, the coach put every senior in. Even though we didn't win, we were out there together and it added significance to the night. I thought it was my last soccer game ever. The junior college I was headed to did not have soccer at the time. It wasn't until my second year there that they established a soccer team. However, during that last high school soccer game and then my last soccer game in junior college, I remember some similar strange thoughts and emotions.

I remember having thoughts of, *What's next? What do I do now?* I don't think it's an exaggeration to say that I was in a place of mourning. Here was something to which I had given decades. Something I had bled for. Something I exerted great energy for. Something I gave time, money, and tears for. Now, it is gone.

Without a doubt, you carry memories of victories with you. Memories of teammates and the comradery are probably my fondest. They remind me that all of the investment was worth it, but it doesn't minimize the sense of loss I have as life on the field fades to memory.

This is why I completely sympathize with professional athletes coming in and out of retirement. I remember people mocking Brett Favre for retiring and un-retiring. But it made sense to me. Of course, Favre achieved a level of athleticism I will never see, and the importance of his decision was far greater than mine, but I got it.

You see, Favre's life was basically four decades of football. For forty-ish years Favre and football were synonymous. He was, and still is, known as a quarterback. Now, he had to leave it all behind. Something that defined him no longer defines him.

Understanding Identity

If I were to ask you, 'Who are you?' How would you answer that? For example, I might answer that by saying, 'I'm a husband to my wife, a father of five, and I work as Director of Resources for Reformed Youth Ministries.' I'm pointing to responsibilities I have in order to convey purpose, significance, and meaning to my life.

For many of us, our occupation is our identity. The lawyer gets great purpose in his life by going to the office. The doctor knows her life has meaning when she helps a patient. The teacher knows his life has value when he can help a student grasp a subject. It makes sense that our occupation influences our identity. That, however, can be dangerous.

In the case of Favre, when he announced his retirement from football, his identity may have been in question. Perhaps this is why he went back and forth on retirement. A primary purpose in his life, which gave him meaning when he got out of bed or walked into a grocery store, was now gone. Who was he if he didn't have football? How would he be identified if he were no longer a football player?

Identity is an exceedingly important reality at the core of humanity. This is something most struggle with, but especially teenagers. The notion of identity hits teenagers primarily at the time of puberty, which is great because nothing adds to the anxiety of puberty like trying to answer the question, *Who am I?*

Teenagers walk down the halls of school wondering what other people think of them. Will they be accepted? What do other people think about when they see me?

Although teenagers may not be consciously asking the question, *Who am I?* they are defining themselves daily. The 'class clown' has discovered that his purpose in life is to make people laugh in class. Maybe this is talking back to the teacher, playing pranks on fellow classmates, or being the center of attention in the cafeteria? Whatever the scenario, he has answered the question.

The 'it girl' at school might answer the question with her appearance. If she begins getting attention for her beauty, she may begin cultivating her image. Although she'll become enslaved to the mirror, to impossible standards, and to the need for external validation, she may successfully establish herself as the 'hot girl'.

And, for the athlete, he has long since answered that question. His name has been equated with speed, ups, and agility. When his name comes up in conversations it is often about how many points he scored that week or how he blew past that defender from the other school. His name has become so 'household' in his context that discussions of him playing on the next level have become very likely.

So likely, in fact, that it was devastating to him and his family when he tore his ACL in the last regular season game. This injury will keep him out of the playoffs, out of the championship game, and out of some opportunities for scouts to consider him after high school. Not only is this tragic, because a player has sustained a serious injury that causes him pain – both emotional and physical – it is tragic because this young man is being faced with this question all over again: *Who am I?*

When I was finally confronted with my last soccer game, I had an identity crisis of sorts. But that should come as no surprise when I spent the majority of my upbringing finding purpose on a field. Those young athletes who sustain major injuries will realize this identity crisis much sooner. Take, for example, the true testimony of this former high school student:

> *I always played sports until I blew out my ankle and had reconstructive surgery. At that point I went from JV volleyball, varsity basketball, and varsity softball to the girl with the blown ankle. The remainder of my high school career I played only volleyball, when I could fit my foot in my shoe. So everything I once identified myself with was gone. I slipped into depression. I started doing drugs and skipping school.[1]*

This may be a more extreme example, but it is not rare. David Elkind also discusses this sense of identity derived from performing in front of an audience. And, as Elkind astutely points out, there are real life audiences and there are imaginary audiences. Children (and adults for that matter) are performing in front of audiences all the time. 'Many child "prodigies" who have been pushed by their parents,' says, Elkind, 'face a "mid-life crisis" in early adolescence when they have to deal with the imaginary as well as the real audience.'[2] This 'mid-life crisis' is the result of a shattered identity.

Every human being is searching for identity. Something to give them purpose and meaning. Something that tells them this is why I'm on this earth, this is why I get out of bed in the morning, and this is where I derive my security. However,

1. Chap Clark, *Hurt: Inside the World of Today's Teenagers* (Grand Rapids: Baker, 2014), p. 119.

2. David Elkind, *The Hurried Child: Growing Up too Fast too Soon* (Cambridge, MA: Perseus Books Group, 1981), p. 137.

whether it's the class clown, the hot girl, the high school athlete or the professional athlete in his retirement, they will all be confronted with this identity crisis, unless their identity is found elsewhere. In a very real sense, the struggle with identity is something that must be stewarded like anything else. As Burk Parsons says, 'To be a steward we must be faithful, and such faithfulness begins with the regular reminder to ourselves … that we are not lords, but stewards, entrusted by God with His Gospel.'[3] Christians must be stewarding their identity by daily reminding ourselves of the Gospel of Jesus Christ.

Securing Identity

Olympic divers David Boudia and Steele Johnson serve as a recent example of a secure identity after their silver medal performance in the 2016 Rio Olympics. Here are two men who've reached the highest goal achievable in their athleticism: the Olympics.

These two young men have spent their lives training for competition. Time, energy, and money have been spent to reach the Olympic Games, and they succeed where many fail. They find themselves competing with the greatest in the world. All their training has brought them to a context, which most human beings will never see. However, they fall short of the gold medal in the Men's synchronized 10m platform and receive the silver.

While this is an amazing accomplishment and something they should be proud of, there may be some who say they failed. That is, their goal should have been gold. There are, no doubt, some who think you only train to win the gold; therefore, anything less should be a disappointment.

There is some validity to this line of thinking. Anyone, Christian or otherwise, should be training to be their best. Christians should be an example of stewardship to the watching world and becoming the greatest in a competition is

3. Burk Parsons, 'Not Lords, Stewards' Ligonier Ministries, March 2, 2011, https://www.ligonier.org/blog/not-lords-stewards/; last accessed February 2018.

one way to display proper stewardship. If a Christian's training can move them to achieve a gold medal, what a witness! While achieving the highest honor in whatever competition should be something Christians strive for, falling short of that goal is not what defines you, as Boudia and Johnson illustrated in Rio.

After earning the silver medal, Boudia said in an interview: 'Yeah, I just think the past week, there's just been an enormous amount of pressure, and I've felt it. You know, it's just an identity crisis. When my mind is on [diving], thinking I'm defined by this, then my mind goes crazy, but we both know our identity is in Christ.'

Boudia gets it. His 'mind goes crazy' when he is defined by his diving. It's not a stretch to use the word 'crazy'. Think of the insanity to place your identity in something that could be taken away so easily.

Using the example of diving, consider the same scenario. Boudia and Johnson have performed hours, days, weeks, months, and years of practice, and while climbing to the platform, one of them falls and breaks a leg. They do not even get to perform what they had spent their lives on. The identity is shattered just like the bone, rendering them hopeless … crazy.

Placing your identity in something so insecure, like athletics, will inevitably leave any individual crazy, fearful, anxious, and depressed. It is madness. Truth be told, this is what many of our young athletes are doing. They are, understandably, finding their identity on the field because much of their lives are given over to sports. Not only that, but also many of these student athletes are actually gifted to play a certain sport. Therefore, the purpose and meaning they derive from the game is that much deeper.

Michael Lawrence helpfully illustrates how this misplaced identity arises in everyday life. 'The … identity markers are more informed by our own background and cultural assumptions than by the storyline of the Bible,' says Lawrence, 'The story of the alien and stranger can become the story of the cultural fundamentalist justifying his disengagement. The story of the bride can easily become the story of self-centered sentimentalism in which, like American brides every Saturday, we are the point and center of it all.'[4] The reality is, when we fail to steward our identity through the gospel, we forget who we are.

Identity Secured

What David Boudia and Steele Johnson realized in the midst of their placing second in the Olympics was that that particular moment, as significant as it was, did not define them. Win or lose, injured or healthy, there was something they could never lose. Something so secure, the gates of hell could never take it away from them. That secure truth? Being a child of God.

An over-arching theme in all of Scripture is that God is faithful to an unfaithful people. Time and time again, God rescues, loves, cares, and protects His people, yet they leave and forsake Him. However, because God promised to love them, He keeps His word … always! Therefore, God sent His Son, Jesus Christ, to live a perfectly obedient life, die an atoning death, and rise to new life. And, by faith in Jesus, I am accepted as God's child.

The apostle John records these words of Jesus:

> *My sheep hear my voice, and I know them, and they follow me.*
> *I give them eternal life, and they will never perish, and no one will*
> *snatch them out of my hand. My Father, who has given them to*
> *me, is greater than all, and no one is able to snatch them out of the*
> *Father's hand.* (John 10:27-29)

When we become Christians, we have an eternity that is secure. We have an identity – child of God – that can never fade away. Not only that, but nothing can 'snatch us' from our Father's grip (John 10:27-29). Not a torn ACL, not failing a math quiz, losing a scholarship, being labeled 'ugly' at school, or never reaching your parent's standards. We are secure, because Jesus

---

4. Michael Lawrence, 'Biblical Theology and Identity,' 9Marks, August 20, 2014. www.9marks.org/articles/biblical-theology-and-identity/; last accessed February 2018.

Christ said, 'It is finished' (John 19:30). He accomplished His task, forever, and no one in history is powerful enough to change that.

To quote Lawrence again:

> *The Father loves the sons [of God] because the Father loves the Son … We can say "God loves you" all day long and it won't make a dent, because people know deep down that God's love is not deserved. But when I'm told that God loves Christ, and that I've been adopted in Christ by faith, I now have something to put my confidence in, something that isn't contradicted by my knowledge of myself.[5]*

Now, this is a message the entire world needs to hear. This is something every tongue, tribe, and nation should rejoice in. More pertinent to this conversation, however, athletes need to hear about this identity in Christ. Athletes, even if they move on to being professional, need to hear this because one day it will come to an end – either due to age, injury or the return of the King.

More specifically, parents must be stewarding their student athlete's identity by clearly communicating this message to them. Their identity is settled with God through their union with Jesus Christ. As Galatians 4 verses 6 and 7 tell us, '… because you are sons, God has sent the Spirit of his Son into our hearts, crying, "Abba! Father!" So you are no longer a slave, but a son, and if a son, then an heir through God.'

Many of our athletes learn hard work through sports, and this is great. But, the identity we have in Jesus Christ is something we cannot earn. The truth of the gospel is this: 'For by grace you have been saved through faith. And this is not your own doing; it is the gift of God, *not a result of works*, so that no one may boast' (Eph. 2:8-9, emphasis mine).

The reality is, Another earned the identity Christians receive by faith. We cannot work to obtain this identity. Jesus already

---

5. Michael Lawrence, 'Biblical Theology and Identity,' 9Marks, August 20, 2014. www.9marks.org/articles/biblical-theology-and-identity/; last accessed February 2018.

accomplished it. By the power of the Holy Spirit, we must steward this identity by daily communing with our Heavenly Father in word and prayer. Wrestling with identity is something everyone struggles with to some degree, so this struggle with identity will be a continuous work of the Spirit. But we cannot earn the right to be a child of God.

While Christian athletes should be the hardest working in the huddle, they must have the understanding that Someone else gave purpose to their life. This, I fear, is a conversation many parents are not having with their young athletes.

According to Kenda Creasy Dean, 'The vast majority of U.S. teenagers are "incredibly inarticulate about their faith"… This was even true for teenagers who regularly attended church … For a striking number of teenagers, the National Study of Youth and Religion interview seemed to be the first time any adult had asked these young people what they believed, and how it mattered in life.'[6]

As Christians, we should be coaching our athletes to work harder than any on the team, but at the end of the day, they must know that they have unending security in the person and work of Christ based on His finished work. Parents must strive to make sure this is a message their children – athletes or otherwise – are hearing consistently in the home, as well as, the pulpit.

※※※※※

After I took off my shin guards and unlaced my cleats one last time, I was confused. I was puzzled as to why it felt like a friend and I were parting company, never to meet again. Why was this sorrow so deep? The familiar smells of the field would fade more and more with time. The routine of drills and various plays would become more distant and fade from memory. The

---

6. It should be noted that this was a combined comment from Kenda Creasy Dean based on statements from the National Study of Youth and Religion and research from Christian Smith. Kenda Creasy Dean, *Almost Christian: What the Faith of Our Teenagers is Telling the American Church* (New York, New York: Oxford University Press, 2010), p. 204.

comrades, who became more like brothers, would become just faces in the hall at school.

Outgrowing a sport is a mournful feeling; that much is sure. Without a doubt, some of these feelings are related to the Fall. That is, we weren't made to grow old. We were made to live and endure for eternity, therefore, outgrowing something because of our age and ability should bring a foreign emotion to the field of play. Although this inner wrestling is an understandable one, our identity should not be in question.

You see, being a child of God ensures I will play again. There will be a day when my body is redeemed, and I will run with greater agility and speed than I've ever known. I will play at a deeper level of greatness and appreciation than is unknown this side of heaven. I will laugh, I will compete, and I will share all of this in community with the Savior who purchased me with His blood. I will play for all eternity – never unlacing the cleats for one last time.

CHAPTER 5

TIME OUT! LOOKING BEYOND THE GAME

*We're all told at some point in time that we can no longer
play the children's game.
… Some of us are told at eighteen, some of us are told at
forty, but we're all told.*

— Scout Barry, *Moneyball* (2011)

IF ever there was a context where time is a dominant factor, it is in the realm of sports. Most of the sports we play have time as a major influencer, evidenced by a large clock on display for all to see. Throughout the game fans and players alike are checking the clock, asking, 'How much time do we have?'

Decisions are made by coaches and players based on the factor of time. Players begin to make plays (or attempt to make plays) they normally wouldn't attempt were it not for time running out. Quarterbacks may force a throw that is typically foolish, but the lack of time justifies it. A basketball player may pull a shot at half court, which would normally give reason for critique were there more time on the clock.

On an average day most human beings don't think about tasks and responsibilities in terms of seconds. How many seconds did you work today? It sounds nonsensical. In sports, however, seconds matter. A second could mean the difference between victory and defeat. Seconds impact the strategy of coaches and players. Seconds make heroes in sports lore. Seconds tell us who the fastest player in the world is. At times a *hundredth* of a second is the only thing that separates gold and silver on the Olympic platform.[1]

---

1. In Brian Edgar's article, *Time for God: Christian Stewardship and the Gift of Time*; The Evangelical Review of Theology (2003) Vol. 27, No. 2.

Time is a common denominator in most every sport. While rules, uniforms, equipment, and seasons may vary, it is time that often remains the dominating influence in the world of sports. More broadly speaking, it is time that separates a 'flash-in-the-pan' athlete from a legend. It is time that determines the legacy an athlete will leave long after they have left this earth. And it is that very thought I want us to have as we think about proper sports stewardship – more specifically, the stewardship of time and how we disciple our young athletes towards this mindset.

When it comes to stewarding the next generation with a proper theology of time, parents and coaches must point their athletes to eternity. Athletes must grow up with a love of the game, but a knowledge that the game is very short in light of eternity. God lays claim of every second we have and our thoughts of eternity assist us in stewarding that.

The Hall of … Faith

The Hall of Fame is something most athletes, even some non-athletes, are familiar with. It is a place for the elite. A place where the legends of a particular sport are enshrined for all to see; those who have accomplished more than many. It is for those who have achieved the respect of their peers – friend or foe – and have attained success, often previously unheard of success, that will find their way into these halls.

Taking a similar mentality from the Hall of Fame, many people label the eleventh chapter of Hebrews as, *The Hall of*

---

he points out the fact that the attention time is getting is increasing in its measurement. 'The digital watch exists as a symbol of the ordering and measuring of personal time in hours, minutes and seconds. What is the time? It is not "rainy season", it is not even Tuesday (measured by days and nights), or "late morning" (measured by the position of the sun) or "about a quarter to eleven" (measured by the sweep of hands on an analogue clock), it is 10:43:07 (measured by the numerical display of a digital watch and accurate to a second or two in a month).' While this attention Edgar speaks of is increasing in our broader culture, the precision of time in the sports world is as much a part of the game as the players.

Fame in the Faith, or some slight variation of that.[2] It is a bit cheesy to refer to this section as such, but many of the 'elites' of the faith are listed in this chapter. Beginning with Abel (v. 4) we are taken through a list of 'super stars' only to run out of time to speak of '… Gideon, Barak, Samson, Jephthah, David, Samuel and the prophets' (v. 32). The Christian reader is taken through redemptive history by the familiar names that are found in many of the popular children's Sunday school lessons.

As we move along this timeline in history, however, we must see that it is God that is faithful. It is God who has sustained the faith of His people. It is God who has worked in all of these individuals, and not people working in their own strength. All of these individuals had a specific amount of time on this earth until they departed. To put it bluntly, it is God who is still acting in history, long after each of these individuals have expired. God is the hero.[3]

In one particular section we read:

> *By faith Moses, when he was born, was hidden for three months by his parents, because they saw that the child was beautiful, and they were not afraid of the king's edict. By faith Moses, when he was grown up, refused to be called the son of Pharaoh's daughter, choosing rather to be mistreated with the people of God than to enjoy the fleeting pleasures of sin. He considered the reproach of Christ greater wealth than the treasures of Egypt, for he was looking to the reward.* (Heb. 11:23-26)

These verses have always left a resonating influence on me. The truth that strikes me the most is Moses' choosing pain.

---

2. Puritan, Richard Sibbes, referred to this section of Scripture as 'a little book of martyrs', according to *The Bible Speaks Today* commentary. Raymond Brown, *The Message of Hebrews* (Downers Grove, IL: InterVarsity Press, 1982), p. 199.

3. See also Raymond Brown, *The Message of Hebrews: Christ Above All* (Downers Grove, IL: InterVarsity Press, 1982), 'The Bible does not seek to mock us when it outlines the achievements of its great characters. It records the truth about them so that, amongst other things, we recognize that they were ordinary people who, by God's grace alone, were enabled to do extraordinary things.' p. 199.

He chose discomfort. He chose affliction. He chose 'to be mistreated with the people of God than to enjoy the fleeting pleasures of sin.' (Heb. 11:26). As Raymond Brown says, 'Life confronts everyone with alternatives and frequently the believer can make a responsible choice only *by faith*. By faith Moses took a series of important decisions by which he cast in his lot with the people of God. By faith Moses abandoned social honours, physical satisfaction and material gain.'[4]

In other words, Moses' view of eternity shaped the way he spent his time on earth. It is this same mindset we read when Moses wrote Psalm 90:12: 'So teach us to number our days that we may get a heart of wisdom.'[5] Our time on this earth is limited, but eternity is forever. Living in light of this assists us in stewarding our time with wisdom.

When we think of professional athletes, we often have a celebrity mindset and because of this they are worshiped as gods. Even Tom Brady and Michael Strahan relayed this through a recent interview discussing their show, *The Religion of Sports*. 'Well, yeah, it really is [a religion]' says, Strahan, 'The temple is the arena or stadium. These athletes can be considered the gods in certain ways and the fans can be considered parishioners. So to be able to explore that and this spiritual connection between sports and life, that's what really piqued my interest.'[6]

Athletes are seen as gods to many, and we pay them as such. To a degree I understand that some of the astronomical amounts they are paid are due, in part, because of the limited length of their careers – many won't play the sport into their mid-thirties. I get that. But many are paid more money than the average human will ever see.

---

4. Raymond Brown, *The Message of Hebrews: Christ Above All* (Downers Grove, IL: InterVarsity Press, 1982), p. 216.

5. I wrote a book based off this verse and you may find it helpful for a biblical understanding of time, *Your Days Are Numbered: A Closer Look at How We Spend Our Time and the Eternity Before Us* (Christian Focus, 2016).

6. Philip Marcelo, 'Brady, Strahan Produce "Religion of Sports" show' *The Clarion Ledger*, September 19, 2016.

What is shocking to many fans is when news reports surface of a particular athlete filing bankruptcy. When that is discovered, the reports often reveal that the particular athlete was very frivolous in their spending and did not plan ahead.

Thinking back to this passage in Hebrews, we read that Moses did the exact opposite when it came to planning ahead. One thing we must realize is that the riches Moses forfeited were far greater than any athlete – he would have had almost anything Pharaoh had. Not only did he abstain from those earthly treasures, he chose enslavement. But he chose it because he was thinking about the future. The verses tell us, '[Moses] was looking to the reward' (Heb. 11:26).

What we know is that the riches of heaven far outweigh those of this fleeting life. Moses knew sin was pleasurable, but those pleasures were fleeting (Heb. 11:25). 'Physical satisfaction was constantly available to Moses in the Egyptian palace, but he identified such pleasures as morally corrupt (sin) and only temporarily enjoyable (fleeting).'[7] To say it another way, sin is fun. It often feels good. This is part of why it is enticing to sin, but any pleasures sin can give you will ultimately leave you feeling empty. You see, sin often blinds us to eternity and gets us to focus on the here and now. Moses knew this and based his entire life on the unfading glories of the next life.

You see, a focus on eternity is exactly how Christians must steward their understanding of time in this life. Time, so often, confines our thinking about our lifespan, but eternity broadens our focus to the life to come.

Eternity and Sports

There is a particular scene in the film *Gladiator* (2000) where Maximus is rallying the troops and he makes this statement: 'What we do in life, echoes in eternity.' There's a lot of truth in that statement. You see, Maximus was doing what any good leader does. He was getting his men to see that they were part of

---

7. Raymond Brown, *The Message of Hebrews*, p. 216.

something bigger. That particular moment would be a moment that had consequences beyond the grave. Many of those men hearing Maximus' voice wouldn't live to see the next day, but he got them to reflect on the significance of the sacrifice they were going to make.

If we are honest, I think our sports are often very nearsighted. Please don't misunderstand me. I am not saying that sports are insignificant or that they have no lasting impression. Without a doubt, I still dwell on games I played in and great games I've attended. I want to be cautious here and reiterate the fact that sports have a big impact on the development of teenagers, but how often are they being used in the development of the child playing? How often are parents and youth workers calling our student athletes – as Maximus did – to think beyond the game and into eternity? Therefore, this critique is aimed more at parents, coaches, and even participants, than it is at sports itself.

As we're thinking about the stewardship of time through sports, it's interesting to think about eternity.[8] I say it's interesting because eternity isn't bound by limitations as time is. Eternity is something vast and unlimited – beyond our understanding. It is forever. But a focus on eternity is essential in our discussion of time, because it shapes our use of time. Perhaps a real-life example would be helpful at this point.

A good friend of mine, who's a pastor at a local church, relayed a story to me about a father who lost a daughter to cancer. His daughter had been sick for quite some time, and it was a rough and difficult battle for the family, as you can imagine. The father made an interesting statement to my friend. He said, 'You

---

8. As one reflects on eternity, it is also interesting to think about eternity past; i.e., before the beginning of time. 'The first words in the Old Testament, "in the beginning…" are the starting point for an understanding of time because, with Augustine, it is best to take this as the beginning of time itself, rooted in the creative activity of God rather than as a description of a creation which takes place in time. Time commences and there is nothing at all in creation "before" this time.' Edgar, Brian. *Time for God: Christian Stewardship and the Gift of Time*. The Evangelical Review of Theology (2003) Vol. 27, No. 2. p. 3.

know how people always talk about quality time being more significant than quantity time? Well, that's not true. Quality time doesn't happen without quantity time.' In some ways this man was expressing regret over the lack of time the family had spent together. It took the death of his daughter to illustrate this truth to him. Quantity time, at least to this man, is more significant than quality time and it seems that quality cannot happen without quantity time.

It seems to me that what we give the most quantity time to is what is often most important to us. For example, if the lawyer doesn't give much quantity time on a case, she will probably lose. If a med student doesn't give quantity time to studying, he probably won't be a doctor. If an athlete doesn't give quantity time to her sport, she will probably never play in college or professionally. If a parent doesn't spend quantity time discipling their child in God's Word, maybe they won't see its value?

You see, I think a view towards eternity shifts our focus on to the soul of a child. In light of the fact that our children's souls will never die, how much time are we spending in their spiritual development? How much of our focus is given to that?

What's interesting is that many Christian families tend to apply quantity time to so much of life, but as soon as that standard is applied to spiritual matters it's seen as legalistic. I've had parents say, 'We don't want to force our child to read God's Word. We don't want to force them to get up a little earlier for a devotion, because it might move them to hate it. They may "burn out" on the faith.' The contradiction, however, is that this same line of thinking is rarely, if ever, employed elsewhere. For example, how many parents say, 'We don't want them to grow tired of calculus, so we won't force them to do their homework. We don't want them to burnout on football, so we'll let them take the year off or skip a couple of practices.'

Andreas Köstenberger gives some helpful advice:

> *In parenting teens … we must teach the need for both spiritual consecration and redemptive engagement with the world, and in that order. Jesus did not send out his followers without first*

preparing them; we likewise must prepare our teens and establish
them in their faith before they can be sent out and act redemptively
toward their peers and others. To send our young people into the
world without adequate spiritual preparation will most likely
yield disastrous results. The spiritual warfare they face is real,
and casualties are high; only the soldier who is prepared will be
victorious in the battle.[9]

As stated, stewarding a mindset of time, through an under-standing of the eternal, helps parents shift their focus to the soul of a child. With a focus on the soul, parents will rightly pursue the 'spiritual consecration' Köstenberger mentions. They will take strides to equip their children to be followers of Christ who are ready to go out into the world.

'[T]oo many Christian parents act as if they do not have time to disciple their children in the gospel story,' says David Prince, 'It is much easier and more efficient to drop them off and allow the "professionals" at the church with seminary degrees to take care of the serious religious stuff.'[10] Often times I think parents don't feel like they have adequate time to disciple their children, because they're carting them all over town to various extracurricular activities. Therefore, they outsource their lack of teaching in the home with ministries the church offers. Don't misunderstand me, it is an absolute must to be connected to the local church, but discipleship in the church should supplement teaching from home, not replace it.[11]

---

9. Andreas Köstenberger, *God, Marriage, and Family: Rebuilding the Biblical Foundation* (Wheaton, IL: Crossway, 2010, 2nd Edition), p. 153.

10. David Prince, *In the Arena*, Kindle edition.

11. Melanie Lacy led a workshop at The 2017 Gospel Coalition National Conference entitled *Engaging Whole Hearts While Forming Young Minds*, in which she said the following, 'We've become particularly good at outsourcing our children ... we're almost putting our children out all the time ... In the UK, at the moment, the average time that a parent spends with their child – in terms of quality time – is thirty-seven minutes per day.' Listen to the full podcast here: https://www.thegospelcoalition.org/podcasts/tgc-podcast/engaging-whole-hearts-forming-young-minds/ last accessed May 11, 2018.

I've been in student ministry well over a decade, and I can tell you that I see many parents apply this quantity method to athletics and academic study. I wish I could say I've seen it when it comes to the spiritual investment in their children. Without a doubt, I have seen parents who make a spiritual investment in their children. I would say, however, that more often than not athletics and academic study take priority over the eternal.

Let me maintain some balance here and say that sports can be used as a window into the soul of a child. For me, sports were a major part of my life, but I often didn't behave like a Christian on the field. Anger and revenge made me play aggressively and, at times, I intentionally injured players. I say that with shame.

What would have been good, however, would have been a discussion of my heart. You see, the anger and aggression that were manifested on the field could have become an eternal discussion on a heart level. Sports, indeed, can be used to invest eternally. They can be, but it seems this type of discipleship isn't always taking place. Even when it is, however, it is no substitution for time under the private and public influence of the eternal Word of God. To be a bit more pointed, children must be under the formal teaching and preaching of the Word in the home and church, so they can learn the informal teaching they receive on the field.

Eternity vs. Sports

While sports can be used to shine a light on the eternal, it often seems that sports and eternal matters are in competition with one another. Competition, however, typically implies that there is a match of equality among those participating. Let me say it this way: If we watch a game involving an inferior opponent playing against a phenomenal team, we may say, 'That wasn't much of a competition'. What we are saying is one team didn't stand a chance against the level of play the other team possessed. Even though dominance can be fun to watch (when it's our team), it is often more enjoyable to watch two equally matched teams compete against one another.

Christians know that eternity is what matters, but it often seems to come in second to sports. Therefore, I might say these two don't seem to be equally matched. At least in our priorities I might say, there doesn't seem to be much competition between sports and eternity.

If living in the South of the US has taught me anything, it is that football is king in the fall. For the record, I love football. If I could pick an ideal Saturday, it would involve grilling out all day long and watching college football. While I enjoy it, and I think Christians can enjoy football, among other sports, any good thing can be abused.

Another lesson I have learned about living in the South and being a youth pastor is this: if I plan an event, I better consult the football schedule. Chad Gibbs, in his equally hilarious and convicting book, *God and Football*, says, 'Churches have to schedule around football … a church event planned on Saturday in the fall is guaranteed to be a colossal failure. So as far as I can tell, the South Eastern Conference does not have to consult churches when it makes the schedule. It makes sense to me that if one thing has to schedule around another, then that thing isn't as important to the people participating.'[12]

When it comes to youth sports, weekend tournaments and Sunday practices typically trump church attendance. The church I am involved in is an excellent church with excellent families. And several of those excellent families are absent many, many Sundays for games and practices. Without a doubt, some of these families do feel conflicted, guilty even, but the sideline devotional or prayer typically salves much of that guilt. However, a devotional about winning the game or a prayer about helping a team play their best doesn't seem to be what Scripture had in mind for the Lord's Day worship.

In fact, a growing trend in sports circles is the abuse of God's Word. 'I have always been somewhat amused but also troubled

---

12. Chad Gibbs, *God and Football: Faith and Fanaticism in the SEC* (Grand Rapids: Zondervan, 2010), p. 14.

every time an athlete quotes Philippians 4:13 right after he or she scores the game-winning touchdown, hits a game-winning home run, nails game-winning free throws, or kicks the game-winning goal,' says Prince, 'Have you ever noticed that no one ever quotes that verse after the game when he or she gave up the game-winning touchdown … It seems that they think about Christ only in relation to their successes as defined by playing well and winning.'[13]

In my local context, I've seen a particular sports ministry that has shortened Philippians 4:13 to a slogan that says, 'I can.' Not only are they abusing God's Word by misapplying it, they have removed Christ altogether.

In Matt Fuller's book, *A Time for Everything*, he discusses the lack of seriousness given to Sundays. Fuller laments:

> *For Christian families, an idolatrous obsession with children is sometimes seen in regularly prioritizing sports clubs or activities over church. It's deeply frustrating that so many sports teams now take place on Sundays, as secular society tries to replace church community with 'touchline community'. Yet it would seem that regularly skipping church to take the kids to football or cricket has gone beyond what's required and drifted into an idolatrous pursuit of time with/for the kids. Your children need Jesus more than they need a professional sports contract. In fact, they need Jesus more than they need to be popular, happy, or thrilled that you are their parents. Similarly, an obsession with tutoring children, so that far more time goes on verbal reasoning or bassoon lessons than on learning of Jesus, is an indicator that loving care may have crossed the line into idolatry.[14]*

Is your sports involvement slipping into over-involvement? Is the commitment to the team rivaling the student's commitment to Jesus Christ? Again, parents and coaches must be stewarding their time better by viewing it in light of an eternity.

---

13. David Prince, *In the Arena*, Kindle edition. He goes on to say, 'A proper understanding of, "I can do all things through him who strengthens me," would lead to quoting it in the midst of athletic failure more often than during athletic success.'

14. Matt Fuller, *A Time for Everything: How to be Busy without Feeling Burdened* (Purcellville, VA: Good Book, 2015), p. 94.

The involvement expected of these young athletes often rivals that of professionals, giving further evidence of quantity time given over to something that should be secondary to their spiritual discipleship. In Mark Hyman's book, *Until it Hurts*, we read, 'Some Little Leaguers ... worked as hard as grown men pitching in big league ballparks. In the clinching game of the 2007 World Series, Red Sox starting (and winning) pitcher Jon Lester tossed ninety-two pitches – one less pitch than those thrown on average by kids who tossed complete games in the 2006 Little League World Series. One overworked lad threw a Nolan Ryan-esque 116 pitches.'[15]

There are many parents that invest inordinate amounts of time at the fields with their children at the earliest of ages, but more studies are showing Early Sports Specialization [ESS] doesn't produce the stellar athletes parents hope for.[16] More often than not, ESS produces burnout or injury in players. Some believe, the idea of ESS really started back in the 1970s after a specific television show seemed to birth this idea.

There was an old television show that ran from the early 60s to the 80s entitled *The Mike Douglas Show*. While many have never heard of that show, I would venture to say that most have been impacted by a particular episode of that show, which aired on October 6, 1978. In fact, this particular show has, most likely, been one of the most significant events to shape the youth sport landscape.

The show was your typical late-night show that featured various celebrities – on this particular show Jimmy Stewart and Bob Hope were his guests – and would often have a

---

15. Mark Hyman, *Until It Hurts: America's Obsession with Youth Sports and How it Harms Our Kids* (Boston: Beacon, 2009), p. 75.

16. In some cases, ESS has been linked to emotional instability among young athletes. Brooke De Lench discusses this in her article, 'Early Sports Specialization Can Interfere with Healthy Child Development, Lead to Social Isolation,' http://www.momsteam.com/successful-parenting/early-sport-specialization-may-interfere-with-healthy-child-development-increase-social-isolation; last accessed February 2018.

novelty piece that highlighted any number of things. For that segment, Mike Douglas thought it would be fun to highlight a two-year old that could hit a golf ball – isn't that cute?! The young tyke hit the golf ball into the air to the cheer and the 'isn't-that-adorable applause' of the audience. Little did this audience know that future audiences would pay good money to watch that little boy – named Tiger Woods – turn golf balls into championship wins.[17]

Getting children early and often seems to be the mantra of youth sports. Young athletes are often at school before many teachers, lifting weights. And, they are typically at school long after teachers have gone home for the day, running drills. By the time they get home, they must hit the books into the wee hours of the night so they can keep the grades. Sadly, there isn't much time left for the reading of God's Word and prayer.

Dr. Timothy Paul Jones makes an astute observation in his book, *Family Ministry Field Guide*. 'If children were a gift for this life only,' says Jones, 'maybe it would make sense to raise them with calendars that are full but souls that are empty, captives of the deadly delusion that their value depends on what they accomplish here and now.'[18] Calendars that are filled with great quantities of athletics and academic study, with some spiritual activities sprinkled in … if there's enough time. Calendars that are filled with quantities of athletic repetition drilled into their bodies, which often leave students too weary to sit through a thirty-minute Bible study.

Students, at least in the Bible Belt in the US, are told to play for the glory of God, but they may struggle to quote one verse of Scripture about God's glory because they rarely have a spare second to crack open a Bible. Again, it's not that these students don't want to be in church or that their parents

---

17. Mark Hyman, *Until It Hurts: America's Obsession with Youth Sports and How it Harms Our Kids* (Boston: Beacon, 2009), p. 16-17.

18. Timothy Paul Jones, *Family Ministry Field Guide: How Your Church Can Equip Parents to Make Disciples* (Indianapolis: Wesleyan, 2011), p. 102.

don't think church has merit, it's simply the way things are structured. Sports have become such a dominating influence that requires so much quantity time that there's not much time for anything else.

It has happened gradually over time; sports weren't this dominant when I played them in the 1990s. Even playing sports on a college level, I know I had more time than many of today's teens and preteens. Just recently I heard a husband and wife lament over the demands of youth sports. So much so, they made the decision to pull their children out of sports for a while. That may seem like no big deal, except for the fact that the wife had played college soccer at a major university, and the husband had played college football at the same university. The two obviously like sports and know they're demanding, but the bar appears to have been raised in just a few years. It seems that the busyness of the sports culture has subtly crept up on parents. And, it's the time-consuming busyness that's blinded us to the eternal.

Parents must recapture a biblical truth that the children's catechism captures. Our children have eternal souls that will never die. In William P. Farley's book, *Gospel-Powered Parenting*, he lists several assumptions parents often make with their children. One of the incorrect assumptions he states deals with salvation. He states that many parents assume their children are saved and he goes on to say that this could be their biggest parenting mistake.[19]

As Farley reminds us, salvation is in the hands of our great God, but God uses parents as the primary disciplers of their children. If we truly believe our children have souls that will live forever, we should be spending quantity time telling them about that eternity. Telling them about the beautiful eternity Jesus Christ purchased for His children. Telling them about a glorious Savior who earned our righteousness through His

---

19. William P. Farley, *Gospel-Powered Parenting: How the Gospel Shapes and Transforms Parenting* (Phillipsburg, NJ: P & R, 2009), p. 26.

obedience, took our punishment by dying on the cross, and then rising again – defeating death – ensuring us that those in Him will rise to new life.

We need to spend great amounts of time telling our children about this truth over and over again. We need to tell them in the morning, tell them throughout the day, and tell them at the dinner table (if you still have one). And, we need to tell them about the eternity that awaits those who don't know this Savior. The point is, we must be using the limited amount of time we have on this earth, to think about the unending nature of eternity and whether or not our children will be there.

CHAPTER 6

BLACK AND BLUE: AN ATHLETE'S GREATEST INSTRUMENT

*My job is to basically beat the s**t out of you for the next five days,
and whoever is still standing at the end, maybe we'll use for our
scout teams. You'll be running the opposition's plays week in and
week out. The greatest value to us is we don't care whether you get
hurt. Our first teams are going to pound on you like you're their
worst enemies. Like what you hear so far?*

— COACH WARREN, *Rudy* (1993)

I CAN vividly remember receiving the ball at our opponent's
midfield. I had just broken past one of their players (I actually
performed a pretty sweet move on their player ... that was
rare for me), discovering that I had an open field in front with
a teammate accompanying me, and a sole defender between us.
Playing on the defense, it was rare to find myself in that position,
but here I was. As I began to dribble toward their goal, my
thoughts were to draw the defender towards me and then pass
it off to my friend who was a much better shot – it seemed clear
that we would most likely get a goal in this moment.

As I drew the defender and began to pass the ball off, he
dove into me, and my ankle completely buckled. I was in a
great deal of pain. I'm not a super-tough guy by any means,
but I had never been injured in a game to such a degree that
I had to leave the game ... until that night. As I tried to get up,
I immediately fell back to the ground, unable to walk. I had to
be assisted off the field. Nothing is worse than having to watch
your teammates finish a game while you're on the sideline ...
unless you have a throbbing injury on top of it.

Fortunately, I didn't break anything, but I was on crutches for a time. Since this injury occurred in college, I had the added bonus of hobbling around campus for weeks. If this were high school, I could have gotten around a bit easier between classes, but college campuses aren't very courteous when it comes to convenience in parking.

Sports and the Fall

I know I learned many lessons from that injury. For starters, I was simply reminded that I could get hurt. I had not previously been injury-prone, and like many athletes, I had forgotten about the possibility of getting hurt. I also encountered daily inconveniences that illustrated how many blessings I took for granted. The most important lesson I learned, however, was this fact – *I was dying.* I'm fairly confident I didn't have that thought at the time, but my ankle injury was illustrative of that biblical truth.

Taking a trip back to the Garden of Eden again, we are reminded that Adam and Eve had a life of perfection. Sin had not yet entered creation; however, when they believed the lie of the devil over the truth of their Creator, death was ushered in. God had warned them of this prior to their eating the forbidden fruit (Gen. 2:17), and after they partook of the forbidden fruit we read, 'By the sweat of your face you shall eat bread, till you return to the ground, for out of it you were taken; for you are dust, and to dust you shall return' (Gen. 3:19).

Gray hairs, wrinkles, aching joints, broken bones, torn ACLs, and sprained ankles all illustrate the fact that we are dying. As Tim Keller says, 'We may use chemicals, cosmetics, and refrigeration to hide from [decay]. The lovely flower today is on the manure pile tomorrow. Natural disaster, famine, disease, decay, mental and physical disabilities, aging, and death itself are the results. Our world, with all of its beauty, is only a dim reflection of what it will be like without sin.'[1]

---

1. Tim Keller, *Ministries of Mercy: The Call of the Jericho Road* (Phillipsburg, NJ: P & R, 1989), pp. 50-51.

Even young teens in the prime of their youth – high metabolisms and all – are dying. Dust serves as an everyday reminder of this. As you hit a couch cushion and send dust particles flying through the air, you are reminded that those particles are human flesh. Our flesh is falling off us because Adam and Eve sinned.

We've seen that sports highlight both the grace and brokenness of life in a fallen world. One area of sports in particular where we see evidence of the Fall is through injuries. We all know that injuries can occur whether or not sports are a part of our lives. For the Christian, however, sports-related injuries are something we must pause and consider.

I remember when I finally decided to play high school football. It was strange because I hadn't played until my senior year, but I had a few friends encourage me to do so – not because of skill or size, I was tall and lanky. On a whim, I signed up just a few days before the deadline.

Part of signing up for this sport included getting a permission slip from my parents. I remember reading over the form and seeing the many warnings of injuries, some even leading to death, which gave me slight pause, but I still signed the form. I also remember my mom handing the form back to me with more hesitation. Everyone knows how rough football can be and injuries are just part of it. With trepidation she approved, expressing her concern for my safety.

Fortunately for her, I was the back-up kicker so I was pretty safe. Yes, I did get to play; yes, I was respected by the team, and yes, I hold the record for never missing a kick. (Okay, so I only kicked three times, and I made two of them. The first was a high snap, which I ended up blocking for our holder and he scored two points.) Even though I was the kicker, injuries were a concern of mine for the simple reason that I was a soccer player. The sport I gave focus to for most of my life was being put in jeopardy because of the possibility of an injury playing football.

Truth be told, however, I could have bypassed playing football to guard against injury that year and still have twisted my ankle walking out the front door. Life in a fallen world means we cannot escape injury even if we abstain from sport. Plus, we must live our lives and not be in fear of possible injuries. While that is true, injuries will remain a constant in sport. Football or foosball, it doesn't matter, people's bodies are decaying.

The Cost of Sports

On the more positive side of sports, one could easily say that sports assist with the stewardship of athletes' bodies. Looking again to ownership, we know that God owns our bodies. Psalm 100 tells us, 'Know that the LORD, he is God! It is he who made us, and we are his; we are his people, and the sheep of his pasture' (v. 3). God owns our bodies so we must steward them out of love for Him. To put it in the negative, it is sinful to simply allow our bodies to waste away from atrophy.

Lack of activity is not only poor stewardship for our students' bodies, but their souls, as well. Paul reminds us of this when he tells us that our physical bodies house the Holy Spirit (1 Cor. 6:19). 'As God's creatures we are not simply souls trapped in human bodies,' says, Vaughan Roberts, 'He made us physical beings; we are *embodied* creatures.'[2] God made us as creatures with bodies and souls, and our physical activity will have an impact on our inner being.

Take, for example, a teenage boy sitting on the couch watching YouTube videos and eating Doritos every day after school. Over time, the physical results of inactivity and unhealthy eating will take a toll on his body. He will grow tired and weak, but that will also manifest itself in a spiritual sense. The lack of self-control he is displaying through his slothful lifestyle will have an impact on his soul. He will, most likely, be feeling too lethargic to read his Bible, for example.

This is where sports can be praised for assisting our student athletes to get off the couch, move around, and use the arms,

---

2. Vaughan Roberts, *Transgender* (UK, The Good Book Company, 2016), p. 38.

legs, and lungs their Creator has graciously given them. That being said, there are some concerns which must be raised when it comes to the topic of stewardship of the body and sports. With all the good sports can do in assisting with the stewardship of bodies, we must weigh the negative.

When we think of the cost of youth sports, I imagine our minds typically gravitate to money. That is definitely a topic that will be addressed a bit later, but consider the physical costs parents pay. The currency of the child's body is what's in focus. Consider this true story:

> *Mary Raine, a sport psychology consultant in Mount Kisco, New York, recalls a family who came to see her colleague Eric Small. The anxious mom and dad wanted the physician's advice about their son, a high school football player. The boy had taken a severe blow to the spleen and hadn't been able to return to the team. He'd come to consult with the doctor on when – or if – he would be able to play football again. After examining the patient, Small called the parents in for a meeting with their son and explained that the injury had been quite serious, and that if the boy played football again he would risk being exposed to another blow, this one life-threatening.*
>
> *The parent's reaction startled Raine. Rather than consider themselves lucky to snatch their son from the football field before something truly awful happened, they searched for ways to keep him in the game. As their son listened, they started negotiating with the doctor. Could their son play with a little padding around his waist? Okay, a lot of padding? 'They didn't want to hear that he could not play football again,' recalls Raine.*[3]

I know that is an extreme case of parents putting their child in harm's way for the sake of a game, but we know the youth sports culture is replete with stories such as this. Scores of parents and coaches are forcing their children to play through injuries, and, truth be told, it is often because the parents and coaches are vicariously living through their children.

---

3. Mark Hyman, *Until It Hurts: America's Obsession with Youth Sports and How it Harms Our Kids* (Boston: Beacon, 2009), p. 24.

Dr. Walt Mueller, President for the Center for Parent/ Youth Understanding, asks the question, 'Who's out on the field?' Mueller is pointing out what so many know to be true: the parent is fulfilling their dream through their child. '[S] ome parents see their kids as a second chance,' says, Mueller, 'to fulfill dreams they themselves never realized.'[4] Many of us know parents like this, and they're easily identified in the stands.

In David Elkind's perennial book, *The Hurried Child*, he posits this insightful thought about a parent's vicarious living. 'I would venture that there is a strong tie between job dissatisfaction, on the one hand, and a disproportionate concern with one's offspring's success in sports, on the other. Children thus became the symbols or carriers of their parent's frustrated competitiveness in the workplace ... [T]he parent soon vicariously invests more of a commitment in the child's athletic life than his or her own work life.'[5]

Without a doubt, the parent living vicariously through their child is one factor that motivates some parents and can be an easy temptation for all of us. The Christian parent, however, must consider the physical cost to our child in the sports in which we enroll. When we know God owns the bodies of our children, what sort of steps must we be taking to steward them faithfully? Let me go a step further and say, are their certain sports Christians shouldn't be participating in? Or, are there aspects of the sports we should strive to change in order to better steward our children's bodies?

For example, Women's Olympic soccer icons, Cindy Parlow Cone and Brandi Chastain, are major supporters of something called *Safer Soccer* [SS]. Part of the focus for SS was started out

---

4. Walt Mueller, 'Kids and Sports ... Lessons Learned from the Land of the Losing,' December 8, 2015, http://www.cpyu.org/2015/12/08/kid-and-sports-lessons-learned-from-the-land-of-losing/; last accessed February 2018.

5. David Elkind, *The Hurried Child: Growing Up too Fast too Soon* (Cambridge, NY: Perseus, 1981), p. 29.

of a concern about concussions among soccer players. One of the goals SS hopes to accomplish is to disallow headers among soccer players below the age of fourteen.

People may think that removing headers from youth soccer is an extreme move, but the fact that 30,000 concussions occur each year in youth soccer and one third of all concussions in youth soccer are from headers, are persuasive statistics. Perhaps Olympic Gold medalist Cindy Parlow Cone is even more persuasive.

Parlow has played on the highest levels attainable in soccer – professionally and in the Olympics. She obviously loves the sport of soccer and knows what she's talking about. Now that she is in her forties, she's beginning to grasp the devastating effects of concussions.

For example, any time she gets behind the wheel of a vehicle, she has to turn on her GPS and enter her destination. Why, you may ask? Inevitably, while Parlow is driving her car, she forgets where she is and where she is going. She must have her GPS because her brain can't remember her destination. The brain God gave her has sustained so much damage through this sport, it won't function properly.[6]

This presents the Christian with a dilemma. If God owns our bodies – brains and all – should parents involve their kids in something that may leave children with lasting brain trauma? God has entrusted the brains and bodies of our children to our care. We cannot be flippant about involving our children in something that can cause lasting impairment to their lives. In a CNN segment discussing the rise of concussions in youth sports, a thirteen-year-old girl was interviewed stating that she takes eleven pills every morning due to concussions. Her athletic career was short-lived as she now is unable to participate.[7]

---

6. *Head Games.* Film produced by Steve James, Variance Films (2012).

7. Tyler Burton, 'Youth Concussions on the Rise Since 2010, Peaking in Fall,' October 11, 2016, http://www.cnn.com/2016/10/11/health/youth-concussions-on-the-rise/index.html; last accessed February 2018.

Here's a diagnostic question for you: If you simply glossed over that previous sentence about a thirteen-year-old taking eleven pills every day, and thought it was no big deal, you might be a bit blinded by your love of the game.

Ultimately, we are talking about involving our children in a sport that could forever alter the quality of life they have. An injury that could keep them from ever being independent from their parents, an injury that could keep them from marriage, or employment or, more importantly, an injury that would keep them from service to the Lord in His Kingdom.

Consider American football. We have become so accustomed to the violence in this sport that labeling it as such may sound a bit shocking (keep in mind that I like football and still watch it). In the documentary, *Head Games*, which analyzes brain trauma in sports, the viewer gets a sobering reminder of what is at stake. The serious effects of concussions are on display in the documentary.

When discussing peewee football, a *neurosurgeon* in the documentary speaks of the foolishness of the concept. Based on the softness of the human skull and the underdeveloped strength of these athletes' necks, he believes these young men have no business playing a game this risky. In his professional opinion, it seemed difficult to say there wouldn't be any lasting effects.[8]

---

8. According to a 2017 study in the *Journal of Athletic Training*, football players suffer more concussions than any other high school athletes. During a game, football players are sixteen-times more likely to suffer a concussion than baseball players and four-times more likely than male basketball players. According to the Centers for Disease Control, during 2005 to 2014, a total of twenty-eight deaths (2.8 deaths per year) from traumatic brain and spinal cord injuries occurred among high school (twenty-four deaths) and college football players (four deaths) combined. Most deaths occurred during competitions and resulted from tackling or being tackled. All four of the college deaths and fourteen (58 per cent) of the twenty-four high school deaths occurred during the last five years (2010–2014) of the ten-year study period. Article, *9 Things You Should Know About Football*, Joe Carter https://www.thegospelcoalition.org/article/9-things-know-football/; last accessed March 22, 2018.

One concern with concussions is how underreported they are. Not only are many student athletes often unaware that they've sustained an injury to their brain, many times they don't want to admit injury in front of their peers. In their attempt to 'suck it up' they play through serious injuries. A 2003 study of the Virginia college football team found that players cumulatively suffered 3,300 'head impacts' over a span of ten games and thirty-five practice sessions. Severe blows were like car wrecks. Typical blows were like a punch to the head. That is the core problem.[9]

I was speaking at a church not too long ago and a parent told me of the pressures to play through injury. He said one of the students at a local high school had been injured and took some time off to recover. While at school, various coaches would pull him to the side and tell him he was letting the team down and needed to get back out there. The boy was nervous walking down the halls of his school due to pressure from these adults. As the parent spoke with me, he said that these coaches were bullying this boy to some degree.

Chronic Traumatic Encephalopathy (CTE) is a related concern when it comes to the discussion of concussions. 'CTE is a progressive degenerative disease of the brain found in athletes, military veterans, and others with a history of repetitive brain trauma.'[10] CTE has become more of a focus in recent years because it is a result of repeated hits to the head that may be milder in form.

Think back to headers in a soccer game or milder head hits in a football game. Over time, this trauma to the brain is leaving people utterly debilitated, unable to function in life. Some instances of suicide have been linked to CTE in the autopsies of high profile athletes.

9. Article, *Time to Push Tackle Football Into Retirement*, by Dan Doriani, https://www.thegospelcoalition.org/article/time-push-tackle-football-retirement/; last accessed March 22, 2018.

10. Concussion Legacy Foundation, www.concussionfoundation.org; last accessed February 2018.

The title of a recent CNN article says it all: *CTE Found in 99% of Studied Brains from Deceased NFL Players.* As you read, it states that CTE was discovered in '110 of 111 brains of deceased former NFL players.' As Dr. Ann McKee, director of Boston University's CTE Center states, 'There's no question that there's a problem in football. That people who play football are at risk for this disease.'[11]

When raising concerns over the physical dangers of sports, I know there would be many who argue that coddling our young children will produce a generation of weaklings. It is important to raise our children with instilled characteristics like discipline, hard work, endurance, strength and fortitude. That being said, it is crucial to hold this entire discussion under the umbrella of stewardship – specifically, our bodies belong to God.

Dr. Dan Doriani says it well: 'I believe the problem of brain damage places football, at the highest levels, in conflict with God's law and character. The Lord creates, protects, and sustains life, but football damages life. Jesus heals, but football wounds. The law says "You shall not kill" and for centuries the church has taken that to forbid all kinds of harm, whether deliberate or careless.'[12]

Half-Time

While there are many parents who cannot wait to see little Johnny return a kickoff at a football game, there are other parents who cannot wait until half-time to see little Bobby play the trumpet. For many, half-time serves as an interruption for their reason to be in attendance at a game. In reality, half-time is a means for coaches and players to reevaluate their strategy. If they're winning, maybe there isn't much to change? If losing, maybe they should go about the game in a different manner?

---

11. www.cnn.com/2017/07/25/health/cte-nfl-players-brains-study/index.html; last accessed March 2018.

12. Article, *Time to Push Tackle Football Into Retirement*, by Dan Doriani, https://www.thegospelcoalition.org/article/time-push-tackle-football-retirement/; last accessed March 22, 2018.

Perhaps the most important reason for half-time, however, is rest. Players are sweating a lot, running a lot, sustaining a lot of turmoil on their bodies, therefore, some water and rest for their muscles can be vital. If players weren't taking breaks at half-time, the likelihood of injuries and dehydration would increase.

The God of the Bible isn't lacking in statements about hard work. He warns about a sluggard mentality and encourages the diligent (Prov. 6:6-11). That being said, He equally encourages rest. He created mankind to work hard and rest – knowing that our rest fuels our work, strength, and creativity.

In fact, before sin even entered the earth, God commanded a day of rest (Gen. 2:1-3). It has become very popular to ignore this command or ridicule Christians who seek to follow it. However, the busyness of our culture, and sports busyness more specifically, are wearing down families. Spouses aren't together, families don't share meals, children are stressed and exhausted to the max. In midst of all the chaos, however, God is calling us to partake of His rest. Scripture teaches that His rest points us to the true rest in Jesus Christ, but, very practically, God also knows our bodies need rest.

Don't take my word for it, however, listen to a professional. John Smoltz, former Atlanta Braves pitcher, in his Hall of Fame speech said, 'Baseball's not a year-round sport.' He went on to say:

> *I want to encourage you, if nothing else, know that your children's passion and desire to play baseball is something that they can do without a competitive pitch. Every throw a kid makes today is a competitive pitch. They don't go outside; they don't have fun; they don't throw enough. But they're competing and maxing out too hard, too early, and that's why we're having these [surgeries on young arms]. So please, take care of those great future arms.*[13]

Smoltz, a professional athlete who excelled in his sport, is telling parents to let their children be children. Elkind also joins in

---

13. See https://www.youtube.com/watch?v=e4MJxW5YC28; last accessed March 2018.

to emphasize this: '[T]he value and meaning of play are poorly understood in our hurried society. Indeed, what happened to adults in our society has now happened to children – play has been transformed into work. What was once recreational – sports, summer camp, musical training – is now professionalized and competitive.'[14]

Let them have fun. Let them play in the back yard. Quit turning everything into a competition or having their free-time shaped by competition. And, I would add, let them rest. This line of thinking, however, goes against the thinking of many parents today.

Thinking back to the function of half-time, I would like to call for a more sustained break. Sports-related injuries are so frequent and so normative, we've seldom stopped to raise any question about them. Broken bones, torn ACLs, and concussions are simply part of life. However, what about injuries incurred on the field of play?

Scripture clearly calls Christians to love the Lord their God with all their heart, soul, mind, and strength. There is cause for concern, however, when there's nothing left for us to give. Many of our student athletes are told to leave it *all* out on the field and give 110 per cent. Yet, do Christian parents take the same fervent mentality towards the spiritual growth of their children?

The structuring of many sports requires all their heart, soul, mind, and strength. If there's anything left over, it is spent on homework – that much is true, I know. Add injuries to the overwork and exhaustion of the future disciples of Christ and they will be too beat up to give much else. If we're talking about a more serious injury to the brain, these disciples of Christ might not have much to offer to His Kingdom, or anyone else for that matter. They won't have the capacity to serve the church or their neighbor.

I understand that all of this is a strong challenge without a clear answer. That being said, we must come back to the issue of

---

14. Elkind, *The Hurried Child*, p. 215.

stewardship. Maybe if our children were truly ours to do what we want with, I would be more likely to brush aside the concern of injury as over-concern. Since our children are God's, that changes things. Since they are to be stewarded to spread His Name to the ends of the earth, this mission is not something we should brush aside too quickly.

Fatigue, overwork, exhaustion, and injury are a few labels that accurately describe the youth sport's culture. I don't think many parents would protest these as inaccurate, and those who would have, most likely, been immersed in the culture too long. Not only do Christian parents need to see the physical stewardship of their children as a biblical call from the Lord, they also need to see a gracious God calling them – and their children – to rest.

CHAPTER 7

THE REAL MONEYBALL

Show me the money!

— ROD TIDWELL, *Jerry Maguire* (1996)

THE film *Moneyball* (nominated for a Best Picture Oscar in 2011) is based on the true story of Billy Beane's (Brad Pitt) efforts to change the game of Major League Baseball. During his time as general manager of the Oakland A's, he attempts to field a team on a tight budget. Realizing the Oakland Athletics are unable to compete with the astronomical budgets of some teams, he bases his team roster on computer-generated analysis of players.

The team initially performs poorly and receives great criticism. Later in the season, however, they begin to perform well and we have the following interchange:

Billy Beane: *It's hard not to be romantic about baseball. This kind of thing, it's fun for the fans. It sells tickets and hot dogs. Doesn't mean anything.*

Peter Brand: *Billy, we just won twenty games in a row.*

Billy Beane: *And what's the point?*

Peter Brand: *We just got the record.*

Billy Beane: *Man, I've been doing this for … listen, man. I've been in this game a long time. I'm not in it for a record, I'll tell you that. I'm not in it for a ring. That's when people get hurt. If we don't win the last game of the Series, they'll dismiss us.*

Peter Brand: *Billy …*

> **Billy Beane:** *I know these guys. I know the way they think, and they will erase us. And everything we've done here, none of it'll matter. Any other team wins the World Series, good for them. They're drinking champagne, they get a ring. But if we win, on our budget, with this team ... we'll have changed the game. And that's what I want. I want it to mean something.*

Without giving away spoilers, I think the fact that *Moneyball* was made into a book and movie is quite telling. Billy's sole objective, at least from the film, was not a ring or even a championship, it was about changing the game. Doing it a different way. Being a pioneer. Having a desire to find greater meaning in the game. After all, he even says it doesn't really mean anything. It's fun and hard not to romanticize it, but it's simply something entertaining. Nothing more than a game.

To quote Jeremy Treat again, he argues that, 'Sports are more than a game; they are part of God's good design for the flourishing of his image bearers as they develop and delight in God's creation.'[1] Treat continues to lay out the graces and curses of sport and illustrates his point well. Sports cannot simply be dismissed as unimportant, but they should not be worshiped as a god; they are somewhere in between – as we have discussed throughout. While Christians agree that sports should not be worshiped as a god, the fact that youth sports is a $7 billion industry seems to illustrate the fact that youth sports has achieved godlike status.[2]

Sports for some is a means of income. Professional athletes make their livelihood from a game. Coaches like Billy Beane are paid salaries to analyze a game, field a team and compete.

---

1. Jeremy Treat, 'More Than a Game: A Theology of Sport,' *Themelios* 40, no. 3 (2015).

2. 'The Finances of Youth Sports in the United States.' Ohio University, https://onlinemasters.ohio.edu/the-finances-of-youth-sports-in-the-united-states/ /; last accessed February 2018. It should also be noted that this $7 billion dollar figure is exclusive to travel or elite sports. When the funds are extended to the youth culture at large, this figure obviously increases.

For those professionals, I'm sure sports become less of a game in the sense that their lives depend upon it for income. Maybe some of the romantic feelings described are lost because of the business mindset that accompanies money. In this context it seems that sports are not a game, but an industry – a business with employees, but not a team.

For others, however, the romanticism for the sport fuels the money spent. I do not doubt that they play for the love of the game, but it may be a misplaced love for the game. Obsession, perhaps, is a more accurate term. I've heard it said before that in order to understand what people truly care about, you take a look at their calendar and checkbook. In other words, you take a look at how people spend their time and money. Well, we've already discussed time – more specifically quality time verses quantity time – but shifting focus to our checkbook, I think it's safe to say that one finds a definite love for the game.

According to Travis Dorsch, assistant professor at Utah State University, the amount of money spent on youth sports has increased significantly and is hurting families.[3] 'The financial cost is easy to see. This weekend, 135 young quarterbacks from thirty-six states will fly to Los Angeles for a two-day camp with Steve Clarkson, a sought-after quarterback coach. Parents of these children, from third through twelfth grade, will pay about $800 each, not including airfare, hotel and other expenses.'[4] It's a modest estimate to state that they ended up spending around $3,000-$4,000 on that one weekend.

When it comes to this kind of spending, I think it is safe to say that people really love sports. However, that love that might be spilling over to obsession, or, speaking in biblical terms, a love that's idolatrous.

---

3. Paul Sullivan, 'The Rising Cost of Youth Sports, in Money and Emotion' *The New York Times*, January 16, 2015, https://www.nytimes.com/2015/01/17/your-money/rising-costs-of-youth-sports.html; last accessed February 2018.

4. Ibid.

I Love You More ...

In my household, we say the words 'I love you' quite often. That's a clear message I want my children to hear repeatedly from me. I don't ever want them to doubt their father's love. Often times, we turn this into a game and my children try to beat me by saying, 'I love you more than you love me!' It has become somewhat of a competition to see who can say it first (Jillian is really good at it).

Well, in Scripture one clearly sees that God the Father loves His children more than they love Him. God tells His children He loves them so much, that none could question His love for His people – even though we do, at times.

The most explicit picture we see of God's love comes from the life, death, and resurrection of the Son, Jesus Christ. Paul reminds us of this when he said, 'If God is for us, who can be against us? He who did not spare his own Son but gave him up for us all, how will he not also with him graciously give us all things?' (Rom. 8:31b-32)

One may debate a lot of things about Scripture – and to be sure there are some things that can be unclear to us – but, one may never call into question the Father's love for His children. It is explicitly clear from Genesis to Revelation. Another thing that's explicitly clear in Scripture from Genesis to Revelation is that God's people love things other than God. God's people turn their backs on Him and worship the creation over the Creator (Rom. 1). They look to *things* for their happiness, instead of the One who graciously gave them those things.

Sport is definitely one of those things that is worshiped as a god. Quite possibly, sports may be the number one false god in all of creation. Maybe it's baseball for some, football (American and otherwise) for others. Basketball, swimming, tennis, golf – you name it, sports find many avenues to our wallets.

When it comes to youth sports, parents aren't passing out million dollar contracts, but some are funneling their income with the hopes for a return on their investment, even though most college scholarships aren't a high return.[5] 'Parents think these investments are justified; they think it will lead to a full ride to college,' says Mark Hyman, 'That's highly misinformed. The percentage of high school kids who go on to play in college is extremely small. In most sports it's under 5 per cent. And the number of kids getting school aid is even smaller – it's 3 per cent.'[6]

Others aren't funding their child's athletics with expectations of professional contracts, but they're still passing funds out left and right. Shoes, socks, shin-guards, jerseys, traveling bags, practice shorts, private lessons, summer camps, league fees, meals on the road, hotels, gas mileage, airfare, cha-ching-cha-ching, money adds up, and one can see that thousands upon thousands of dollars are being spent on youth sports during multiple seasons a year. Based on the previous chapter, doctor's visits, physical therapy, and medical treatment should be added to the list of accrued expenses. Youth sports are never, ever cheap.

However, what exactly are parents spending money on? Let me say it this way. Scripture gives many warnings and much instruction on money. Possibly the most familiar verse warning about money comes from Paul's first letter to Timothy: 'For the love of money is a root of all kinds of evils. It is through this craving that some have wandered away from the faith and pierced themselves with many pangs' (1 Tim. 6:10).

Paul's warning here should give us great pause. He's saying that there are those whose love for money is so great that they trade the Kingdom of God for this life. They love money to such a degree that they become blinded to eternity, blinded to their soul, and blinded to the destruction that's in store for them. In short, the love for money can be *extremely* intense.

---

5. Many parents obviously hope for an athletic scholarship, even though most scholarships do not cover the amount of tuition. Mark Hyman claims that most scholarships only cover a fourth of the cost of tuition. Mark Hyman, *Until It Hurts: America's Obsession with Youth Sports and How it Harms Our Kids* (Boston: Beacon, 2009), p. 34.

6. Paul Sullivan, 'The Rising Cost of Youth Sports, in Money and Emotion.' The New York Times. Ibid.

Here's my point: if love of money is so powerful that it could blind us to this degree, what greater love is moving people to throw thousands of dollars at youth sports? What is driving parents to write check after check towards athletics? What is it about youth sports that are, in some cases, moving parents to spend anywhere from 10 to 20 percent of their income?[7] In my experience, parents often – without hesitation – give to anything if it's sports-related. Stadiums are built, gyms are funded, programs are started, jerseys are paid for, booster clubs are formed. Sports get money when needed.

The church, on the other hand, has to start a multi-year capital campaign. They have to carefully communicate to the congregation or people will leave the church. They have to carefully and graciously craft their words in order to guard against offence. To be sure, the pastor and leaders must be careful with the handling of money, because it belongs to the Lord after all. They should be wise and slow with the spending of resources, but contrast the churches' careful approach with sports-related spending.

It once again comes down to a stewardship issue. Money possesses a power over people, and it seems that sports have tapped into something that makes money very easy to let go. Therefore, what is driving sports-related spending?

Child-Centered Home

Let me go ahead and state the obvious, our children are driving this money. It takes no genius to see that children are the driving factor for youth-related sports, but my point is more narrowly focused on the love of our children. Let me get a bit more pointed by saying the idolatry of our children.

Satan is very crafty and he works very subtly. Seldom will he come to us as a wolf, but often he comes as a wolf in sheep's clothing. It seems that here, Satan has taken a wonderful, beautiful, joyous gift like children and turned it into idolatry.

---

7. 'The Finances of Youth Sports in the United States.' Ohio University, ibid

One time I was asked to speak at a church out of town. One of my friends was the pastor there, and he was going to pick me up from the place I was staying. When he picked me up, one of his children was riding with him and got out of the front seat in order to allow me to sit there. As the child was getting out, I attempted to stop them, and said that I could sit in the back, but they unflinchingly opened the door to the backseat and climbed in. My friend was motioning me into the front seat during this interchange and as I climbed in he said to me, 'My child knows their place.'

To be clear, my friend's candor was in jest, and for the record his child thought it was funny, too. But, what he followed up with was this truth. You see, my friend had been a missionary outside the United States for years. He informed me that overseas, children are not worshiped like they are over here. Children (for the most part) do not question their authority, and children are clearly taught who is in authority. Therefore, this child knew that 'their place' was in the backseat when there was an adult passenger.

Working in student ministry for well over a decade, I'm not quite sure American children have gotten this message. To be sure, there are plenty of parents who exercise authority and communicate respect to their children, and I'm so glad to say that the parents in the ministry I lead have sought to teach this. But there are many more who do not. In the child's defense, when the parent's calendars and checkbooks are arranged around them, what do we expect to happen? When children become entitled and demanding, that is more of a parenting issue, and responsibility is squarely placed on their shoulders.

Another story to illustrate what I'm talking about. One time I was over at a family's house as one of their children came in from a certain sports practice. As the fatigued, working mother came in with her child, the child plopped down in a chair. While the mother was beginning to make preparations for supper, the child (I am not making this up) said, 'Untie my shoe.' Not, Please untie my shoe, mother, or even the question,

Could you untie my shoe? As if a parent untying the shoe of a child wasn't insulting enough, the child expressed it in a command. To my complete shock, the mother did not hesitate to get on her knees and untie this child's shoe. Who was in the place of authority in this situation?

Yet again, I fault the parents here. They taught this child who's in charge. The checkbook and the calendar revolved around this individual. This child was simply living out the worldview they had been taught. That worldview? The household is centered on the child. Without a doubt, the child-centered home is cause for many families spending money on their athletic endeavors.

Chasing a Dream

Life is an amazingly beautiful, complex thing. I think it's normal to say that most human beings have great aspirations to be someone or do something extraordinary. But, if everyone did something extraordinary, it would cease to be … *extra*ordinary. Sort of like a conversation that takes place in the Pixar film, *The Incredibles*.

Helen, a.k.a. *Elastigirl*, is talking with her son Dash. Dash wants to 'go out for sports.' Helen's reluctance is due to the fact that Dash has the superpower of speed. As the discussion draws to a close, Dash says, 'But dad always said our powers were nothing to be ashamed of, our powers made us special.' Helen replies, 'Everyone's special, Dash.' To which Dash responds: 'Which is another way of saying no one is.'

If everyone were uniquely gifted with speed, like Dash, it would cease to be unique. Similarly, if everyone could make it to the NFL, NBA, or MLB, it wouldn't be much of an accomplishment. Yet, it seems to be these dreams that motivate much of the athletic pursuits of family, even though one stat tells us that every year only two hundred of the thirty million youth sports participants will make it to the next level.[8] However, as

---

8. H. G. Bissinger, *Friday Night Lights: A Town, a Team, a Dream* (Boston: Da Capo, 1990), p109. In Paul Sullivan's Times article previously quoted he

mentioned earlier, it seems that much of the extraordinary is being pursued by the parents and not the students.

In a New York Times article, Paul Sullivan, talks about three different professional athletes in the NBA, the MLB, and the NFL. He goes on to say, 'These men represent the dreams of many children – and more often their parents ... [T]hese three athletes, now in their 30s and 40s and from different backgrounds, agree on one thing: The way youth sports are played today bears no resemblance to their childhoods, and the money, time and energy that parents spend is probably misplaced.'[9]

Through my years of student ministry, I've spoken with more than a handful of students who are tired of their sport. They lament the practices, the amount of time, which often leads me to ask them if they even enjoy the sport – some do, some don't. To be sure, some of their dislike is due to a lack of discipline and drive, which sports can assist in dissipating. Even so, there are those students who are simply in the sport to appease their parents.

One athlete finally admitted his lack of love for the sport that made him famous. 'I play tennis for a living even though I hate tennis, hate it with a dark and secret passion and always have.' Those are some pretty strong words. 'Hate it with a dark and secret passion.' The strength of those words increase when we discover that they were spoken by Andre Agassi, lamenting the utter dominance a sport takes over your life.[10]

---

quotes a private coach saying, 'What I hope parents understand is that there are some three million high school players and by the time they scale that down to the quarterback position there are a couple of hundred thousand starters. Then you get to Division I and II, and there are 360 quarterbacks. When you get to the NFL there are 64. When you think about the odds, that's not very good odds.'

9. Paul Sullivan, The New York Times. Ibid.

10. This quote appeared in The Guardian article, *Why Did Andre Agassi Hate Tennis?* This was an excerpt from his book, *Open*; https://www.theguardian.com/sport/2009/oct/29/andre-agassi-hate-tennis; last accessed March 2018.

Yet again, there are some parents who want to utilize sports to instill a team mentality or discipline or simply have fun, I understand that. One of the most enjoyable aspects of playing sports for me came from being a part of a team. However, there are those parents who had dreams to accomplish something extraordinary, and they never did. Even though they came up short of their dreams, their child can help them accomplish this.

Could chasing down this dream be an explanation for the amount of money being poured into youth athletics?

Caught Up in the Crowd

At a 2014 *Together for the Gospel* pastor's conference, Dr. John MacArthur spoke about Jesus' public ministry.[11] At one point he talked about the crowds of people that followed Jesus. His point in discussing the crowds that followed Jesus was to say that many of the people in the crowds didn't necessarily love Jesus or follow Him because they were persuaded by His teaching. They followed Jesus because that's what everyone else was doing.

At this point MacArthur simply pointed to the fact that people are drawn to crowds. He basically said people merely go where people are. If people are there, that's where we want to be, and we get the sense that we're missing out if we're not there.

On Friday nights in many towns, stadiums are packed with people. In some towns, everything shuts down for the 'Friday Night Lights.' The crowds are there, so that's where we'll go. The same is said of the college football experience – that's where the crowds are.

Crowds attract us more than I think we often realize. When it comes to youth sports, I think this is much of the draw. Crowds of people are at the soccer fields, the tennis courts, the track meets, the dance recitals, the fill-in-the-blank. Since we

---

11. John MacAurthur, *Mass Defection: The Great Physician Confronts the Pathology of Counterfeit Faith*. Together for the Gospel Conference: Lousiville, KY, April 2014.

are attracted to crowds, and we want to be where the people are, this justifies the amount of money we spend. Being surrounded by the crowds eases the conscience when it comes to spending money, because it makes us feel important to be surrounded by so many. It gives us the illusion that we aren't missing out on life, because we are with all these other people.

There is another aspect to this and that is being left out of the crowd. When it comes to a parent's love for a child, they rightly want their child to fit in and be accepted among their peers.

Bob Cook, in an article that appeared in Forbes, points to a peer pressure among parents that feeds the spending. 'Parents often spend money not because they are driven to get their kid a scholarship,' states Cook, 'but because they fear what might happen (their child's future failure to make the high school team, parent ostracization) if they don't. And the more affluent the area, the more those fears intensify ... [P]arents, no matter their income level, feel that they are prisoners of a system that demands the only way to have a child who doesn't grow up to be selling pencils on street corners is to shovel mass amounts of money into intense youth activities at ever-earlier ages.'[12]

In, *The Hurried Child,* David Elkind discusses this fear when he says, 'When most of the parents in the community have their children on a soccer team, in Little League, or ballet, there are no playmates left for the child who does not participate. Unless the child is enrolled in comparable programs, there is no one in the neighborhood to pal around with.'[13] There's no one to 'pal around with' because the crowds have left the neighborhood and populated the athletic fields. This results in the 'parental

---

12. Bob Cook, 'What Drives Parents' Youth Sports Spending? Don't Underestimate Peer Pressure.' Forbes August 1, 2016. https://www.forbes.com/sites/bobcook/2016/08/01/what-drives-parents-youth-sports-spending-dont-underestimate-peer-pressure/#70c34a247325; last accessed February 2018.

13. David Elkind, *The Hurried Child: Growing Up too Fast too Soon* (Cambridge, ST: Perseus, 1981), p. 31.

peer pressure,'[14] Elkind later discusses. The fear is that their child will miss out and that serves as motivation for their child's participation and the dollars that follow.

We Are Rich

I remember watching the old show, *Lifestyles of the Rich and Famous*, when I was a kid. As I got a bit older, MTV had a similar show called, *MTV Cribs*. The essence of these shows was to display the disgusting riches of some of the wealthiest people this side of heaven. As you watched the show, you were taken on a tour of their house and shown most of their prized possessions.

I remember a specific episode of *Cribs*, where some rich and famous guy was showing off his shoe collection. He had a closet that would rival the size of my first house with floor-to-ceiling shelves filled with shoes. As he was showing off these shoes, he told the viewing audience that he only wore each pair *once*. Read that again and let it sink it. He explained that he would wear a pair of shoes one time and then the 'freshness' would be gone, so he wouldn't wear them again. It was repulsive to watch such waste and be unmoved by it.

Well, we may not have a shoe closet anywhere near that size, but we are rich. I don't know you personally or anything about your lifestyle, but chances are you're rich compared to much of the world. Without a doubt, you could be in some dire financial providences that are difficult, but if you had enough money to purchase this book, you're probably doing okay.

I've heard of celebrities who vowed to live off of one dollar a day, because many in the world live on less than that. The celebrities were trying to raise awareness of the utter poverty much of the world lives in. This is what I mean by stating that you're rich; you're not one of those people. Chances are, you have running water and electricity, four walls and a roof, and you probably aren't concerned about eating today. That's not

---

14. Ibid., p. 32.

the case for everyone in this world. There are many shoeless children with blistered and crusty feet who'd love to have one of the aforementioned 'unfresh' pairs of shoes discarded by the money-hungry celebrity.

Tim Keller gives a wise answer when considering how much of our income we should give away: 'Be sure that you're giving cuts into your own lifestyle so that some of the burden of the needy falls on you. Then, look at your own family's gifts and ministry opportunities and find the calling God has for you. Every person and family must minister in mercy. God calls some people to more extensive ministries by giving them desire, ability, and opportunity. Finally, be sure you provide for your own family so that neither they nor you will be a burden or liability to others. Beyond that, trust in God.'[15]

In the midst of the excessive earthly riches we've been given, we've often forgotten what it's like to go without. We have so much stuff, we have to purchase more buildings called storage sheds to store our stuff. Further, in this excess, we often spend more than we should. Sports become a likely outlet, because they are a good thing.

Perhaps the affluence we've been given is part of the reason we spend more than we often should on youth sports?

Nothing is more unpopular than a guy writing a book critiquing sports. Unless that same guy adds a critique of the way Christians spend money. Even so, filtering all of this dialogue through the lens of stewardship is crucial. When we truly believe God is the owner of our lives, our time, our bodies, and our money, that changes everything. Maybe I could use a personal example that isn't related to money.

I try to steward the body God has given me by exercising (I need to work on my eating habits). I struggle to know how much is too much at times, and I question my heart motives, but I know God owns my body and I need to take care of it.

---

15. Tim Keller, *Ministries of Mercy: The Call of the Jericho Road* (Phillipsburg, New Jersey: P & R, 1989), p. 78.

Well, over the past year, I have injured myself multiple times. This has been incredibly frustrating. And part of the frustration is due to the fact that I'm unsure how I got injured. From my perspective, I've tried to guard my body from injuries by exercising, but I've actually received injuries.

During my last injury, I pinched a nerve in my C7 vertebra, which led to no feeling in some of my fingers in my left hand. For well over a month, I had no feeling and little to no arm strength in my entire arm. Initially, I could hardly turn the steering wheel of my car with that arm. Everything I worked hard to gain was now gone. My frustration led to anger and bitterness. *What's the point?!*, I thought. I've spent all this time trying to get in shape and all it's gotten me is physical therapy and spending money I don't have. I was angry. Plain and simple.

God, in His grace, however taught me something. He taught me that I was angry at … *Him*. My frustration and anger over the lack of feeling in my fingers was actually directed towards Him. Why was it directed towards Him? Because He's the sovereign King over all creation. He's the Owner. To say it another way, it was His will to usher that bitter providence into my life. In my anger I was, in essence, saying, God, you owe me feeling in my fingertips. I deserve to have use of my arm.

I was reminded that God doesn't owe me anything. Not only is He completely just and good to take feeling away from my fingers, He would be completely just and good to take away my entire arm … or legs … or whatever He chooses, because He *owns* me!

Just as God owns me and everything about me, He owns my money. Every dime I have belongs to Him. The question for Christians is: are we spending our money in a way that reflects God's ownership? Do we understand that every dime we own ultimately doesn't belong to us? Are we spending our money in a way that builds our little kingdom or God's kingdom?

When it comes to youth sports, Christians must be spending their money in a way that's different from the world. Christians must search their hearts and ask why they often give money so freely to sports but reluctantly to the church. Christians must be convicted over their lack of stewardship in this area and repent at the exorbitant amounts they often give to youth sports. This will only occur when we grasp the truth that every dollar in our bank account was graciously given to us by our Heavenly Father.

As I once heard John Piper say, 'You were blessed to be a blessing.' God has blessed you with money, so you can be a blessing to others. The old adage – Money can't buy happiness – is indeed true. However, there is so much need and so much pain in this world and it is very true that money can alleviate much of that pain. Christian, are you using your money to be a blessing to others?

CHAPTER 8

COMING IN SECOND

I think if I was an Olympic athlete, I would rather come in last than win the silver, if ... you know, you win the gold, you feel good. You win the bronze, you think, well, at least I got something. But you win that silver, that's like congratulations, you almost won. Of all the losers, you came in first of that group. You're the number one loser.

— JERRY SEINFELD, I'm Telling You for the Last Time (1998)

IT hurt. There was a definite pain, but it wasn't really a physical pain. To be sure, the hurt was felt but it was different than breaking a bone, spraining an ankle or pulling a muscle. Those injuries can be excruciating, but this was a different category of hurt that was equally agonizing in another way. You couldn't ice this hurt. You couldn't wrap it in tape. You couldn't go see a doctor or receive treatments from a trainer. This was the pain of losing.

It's a pain that lingers. There is the initial pain that comes with any loss, but then there's the secondary pain. There's the pain that takes place in reflection. If I had run a little faster, thrown the ball earlier, swung later, passed it instead of pulled it – all the 'what-ifs' flood the mind and add to the pain.

Any athlete who competes long enough tastes this pain. In some ways, the pain and discomfort of losing fuels the passion to win. The bitterness of defeat only spurs the best on to win.

Losing is unnatural to us, because we weren't created to lose. Feelings of loss and emptiness were ushered in by the Fall. Think of it this way: when you hear a person say that someone died of 'natural causes,' that's inaccurate. Now, of course I get what they mean, and I'm not encouraging you to correct someone when they say this – especially in the context of death – but death is unnatural. Human beings weren't created to die. Sin ushered in the harsh, unpleasant reality of death.

That being said, losing is a part of competing. Players enter any competition with the understanding that a loss could await them at the end of the game. It is this knowledge of losing that often spurs athletes along to play better and compete on a greater level. However, there are various sports leagues – sadly many of them are 'Christian' leagues – that do away with losing. They have structured a league that omits one victor and one loser – nobody wins, but nobody loses. To be fair, I'm sure the league is attempting to properly care for their children, but this model is not helpful. 'Though not keeping score and handing out participation trophies in youth sports is often passed off as a Christian idea,' says, David Prince, 'the root of this kind of thinking is found in modern psychological theory and not in the Bible.'[1]

It seems that these leagues have reacted in the extreme to the uncomfortable emotions that accompany losing. While feelings of loss might be a result of the Fall, removing the threat of losing takes away God-honoring competition that spurs athletes on to be their best.

In a similar vein, losing is something that will always be bitter and never easily accepted, but there is 'healthy losing' that's beneficial to any athlete. There are those losses a team or individual may receive from a far superior team or athlete. In those moments, greatness can be appreciated and the loss is more easily stomached. It is also an example the defeated opponent can look to for instruction. *They were the better team,* can be something more than a sentiment from a player in a post-game interview. It may be spoken from a sincere heart, appreciating the talents of another.

That being said, to quote Seinfeld, coming in second is just another way of saying, 'You're the number one loser,' and it

1. Prince, David E. (2016-08-16). *In the Arena: The Promise of Sports for Christian Discipleship.* B&H Publishing Group. Kindle edition.

just plain hurts. It is this idea that makes Ted Kluck loath the Olympics. 'I hate [the Olympics]. I can't watch them because the Olympics are about being perfect. There's the winner, and then there's everybody else. There is something about watching someone's dreams die that just makes me sick... [they are] world class... and all but three lose.'[2]

As we think about losing and the pain that accompanies it, we also need to understand that there is, at times, a certain level of entitlement one may feel. Most athletes wouldn't say this, but there's probably the thought of: I deserve to win. How dare this other opponent consider taking this from me?

Some may rush to judgment over thoughts of entitlement, but I think it's understandable. Consider athletes on a collegiate or professional level; they have given so much time and energy to their sport. Therefore, the loss hurts all the more, not only because they worked so hard, but also because we have the firm belief that hard work yields results.

For example, if an employee works harder than anyone in the office, a wise boss would honor that employee. Their hard work should serve as a motivator to others in the office. Therefore, the employer recognizes their work in order to instill that attitude in others.

That being said, even though losing hurts, it is quite healthy for anyone. In reference to the prideful heart of a teenage athlete, a good dose of humility will do them good. The self-esteem age is sending a message of believe in yourself as a winner and it will happen. 'If feelings of self-esteem are the key to success in life,' Prince says, 'the thinking goes, then every child must be told he or she is a winner, and handed a trophy, even when he or she loses ... Our culture says, "Believe in yourself," and Jesus says, "Deny yourself and follow me" (Luke 9:23). No one can do both.'[3]

---

2. Ted Kluck, *Household Gods: Freed from the Worship of Family to Delight in the Glory of God.* (Carol Stream, ST: NavPress, 2014), p. 95.

3. Prince, David E. (2016-08-16). *In the Arena: The Promise of Sports for Christian Discipleship.* B&H Publishing Group. Kindle edition.

When athletes work hard only to be defeated, it is quite deflating. If they come in second, it's almost likened to no recognition for all the hard work. Feelings of despair and thoughts of 'what is the point?' begin to creep into the mind. I deprived myself of rest, I deprived myself of eating certain foods, I put blood, sweat, and tears into this. In other words, I have sacrificed so much for this game only to see the recognition go to another.

Therefore, what sort of stewardship of praise or acclaim are Christian athletes to display on the field? How are Christian athletes supposed to steward the emotions of winning and losing in competition? Is there room for them to boast in their accomplishments? Is there a time to mourn their loss? How do Christian athletes best steward these emotions in a Christ-like manner?

Recognition

While it is nice to be the champion in a sport and receive a pat on the back for excelling, what is it we're really celebrating? To be sure, Super Bowl, World Cup, or World Series champions are celebrated for their skill. With all the confetti and the parades comes an appreciation for the hard work of these competitors. Fans are giving one big 'Thank You' for representing 'their team.' Whether their team is a city or a country, fans are boasting in the success. If we get down to the core of this excitement, however, more often than not, I think we can see that pride is a major emotion the Christian should be cautious about.

Players want to work hard to compete to their maximum potential, but the praise of man must be a sincere caution because of the temptations that accompany it. To be recognized as the best or the champion before mankind fuels the desire to win. The praise of man is a high-powered, feel-good, driving force for much of what we do. In short, men and women love the praise of other men and women.

Speaking personally, I remember loving to play in front of a large crowd. Without a doubt, there was more pressure to play before a larger audience, but it also increased the 'high' of winning. Conversely, I remember playing games in front of a smaller audience and being disappointed. If I'm honest, it was because of my pride. I wanted more people in the stands to see me and my skills (which weren't anything too special).

Why do you think Jesus Christ warned us about the praise of man so much? He warned of this when being charitable: '… do not let your left hand know what your right hand is doing' (Matt. 6:3). Jesus spoke on this when teaching how to pray: 'But when you pray, go into your room and shut the door and pray to your Father who is in secret' (Matt. 6:6). To be sure, there can be public prayers, but Jesus was cautioning our recognition-seeking hearts. He gave the same caution about fasting: do not do it for recognition (Matt. 6:16-18).

To the contrary, Jesus condemns the Pharisees for 'they loved human praise more than praise from God' (John 12:43 NIV). Jesus is clear to tell us that when you announce your giving to charity or pray before men or fast in a self-seeking way, you have received your reward (Matt. 6:2, 5, 16). Part of Jesus' point, however, is the fact that there is a reward. When we do something for others to see and recognize, it feels good when they do. The reward, however temporal it may be, feels so good in the moment.

Whenever I see a celebrity – athlete or otherwise – doing a bunch of good in front of a bunch of cameras, I can't help but be a little cynical. Of course you're doing good when the cameras are rolling. To be fair, many of those celebrities try to hide from the cameras, but they are followed wherever they go. That being said, we all know there are plenty of 'charitable moments' that are merely good PR. Such moments are simply for the praise of man, and celebrity athletes receive a reward for it. It increases their brand, gets them better marketing, more followers on Twitter or Instagram.

Contrast all this recognition with the Man of Sorrows. One of the most significant Scriptures that illustrates this is Philippians 2:5-11:

Have this mind among yourselves, which is yours in Christ Jesus, who, though he was in the form of God, did not count equality with God a thing to be grasped, but emptied himself, by taking the form of a servant, being born in the likeness of men. And being found in human form, he humbled himself by becoming obedient to the point of death, even death on a cross. Therefore, God has highly exalted him and bestowed on him the name that is above every name, so that at the name of Jesus every knee should bow, in heaven and on earth and under the earth, and every tongue confess that Jesus Christ is Lord, to the glory of God the Father.

This is the epitome of humility. It is humility beyond our finite understanding. Jesus Christ had riches we cannot fathom. Jesus Christ had peace we cannot fathom. Jesus Christ had joy we cannot fathom. Jesus Christ had all of that and much, much more and laid it aside for His children.

Jesus Christ had the most glorious throne beyond our comprehension, but He laid it aside to be born in a filthy, feeding trough. A trough where snotty, muddy, snouts of pigs feasted. Jesus descended from a place of supreme recognition to a place of obscurity.

Without a doubt some people recognized Jesus as the Son of God at His birth, but He came to this earth to love a people that could *never* give Him the recognition He deserves. And, even though He is exalted and is worshiped by millions upon millions and every knee will bow; those who love Him are still unable to love and worship Him in the way He deserves. They are incapable of fully recognizing Him as the King of kings in the manner of which He is worthy. Truth be told, His followers will spend the rest of eternity grasping His glory and seeing new facets of it with each passing eternity.

It is impossible for fallen human beings to grasp the recognition that was due to our Savior, Jesus Christ, yet He laid this recognition to the side and was born in a feeding trough. Jesus lived in utter obscurity for the vast majority of His life. He was the King of the Universe, but worked quietly as a carpenter. What applications can be taken from this into the realm of sports?

Humility

C. S. Lewis' section on humility in his work, *Mere Christianity*, is among the greatest reflections of humility. Lewis says, 'If anyone would like to acquire humility, I can, I think, tell him the first step. The first step is to realize that one is proud. And a biggish step, too. At least, nothing whatever can be done before it. If you think you are not conceited, it means you are very conceited indeed.[4] That is to say, humility is putting another before self, which is quite unnatural to the prideful heart of man. For one to be humble, they must first realize that they are not.

As I write this, there has been a trending story in college football about a charitable act of a certain player at Florida State University. Wide receiver, Travis Rudolph, was visiting a nearby middle school in Tallahassee when he noticed a young man, Bo Paske, sitting alone in the cafeteria. Rudolph decided to reach out to Paske by sitting with him during lunch. Rudolph was unaware that Paske has autism. Rudolph simply knew what it was like to go through middle school. He knew the loneliness and lack of love that is so often present. He knew these difficulties and made a small gesture that attempted to alleviate some of them in this young man's life. Moved by compassion, he reached out to show love to another.

I think Rudolph is an excellent example of humility. Rudolph is great in the eyes of the world. He's successful and admired by fans – he has fans, for that matter. Yet, he enters into another young man's life that is viewed as less important in the eyes of the world. While Rudolph has athletic abilities of greatness, this young man does not. His autism has actually isolated him from many. The only followers he has are obscurity and isolation.

This is, no doubt, an admirable action by Rudolph. It's an action that brought me to tears, and I applaud him for it. Where the illustration breaks down, however, is in the fact that Travis Rudolph is just as broken as Bo Paske. Rudolph may have talents unlike many, but he's a sinner in need of God's grace just as much as Paske ... or you or I. It is this notion that can guard us from idolatrous, hero-worship that's often associated with

---

4. C. S. Lewis, *Mere Christianity* (New York: Harper Collins, 1952), p. 128.

sports. The truth that all of us are broken sinners in need of God's grace, can foster the humility Lewis spoke of.

We all have notions of greatness, and athleticism rises to the top in many eyes. However, Jesus Christ possessed true greatness. Yet, He laid His greatness to the side to dwell with a broken people in a broken world, possessing a body that could bleed and die like yours and mine. Scripture says, '[Jesus Christ] … came not to be served but to serve, and to give his life as a ransom for many' (Mark 10:45).

Contrast the mindset of Christ with much of the pride that's associated with sports. If we are discerning, we can see that much of their structure has been built on the worship of self. They are often antithetical to the humble, service-minded example Christ left us. If we call ourselves Christian, a servant heart is not optional. To claim the name of Christ, we must die to self and serve others. Just as losing is unnatural, service is as well. Service is an unnatural thing for a fallen heart. That is to say, if we just let our heart pursue its natural bent, self-worship will be the outcome.

To be sure, there are celebratory moments Christians can, and should, join in through sports. There should be times of utter astonishment at athletic displays on the field. While all that is true, the Christian athlete and spectator must have a grasp of the pride that's easily manifested in a sinful heart.

I know many will recoil at a statement which labels sports with pride, but I think much of that is due to the familiarity we have with sports. We've become so accustomed to the world of sports that our eyes don't even see the pride that is present. As we consider some of the following examples, I want to be cautious of swerving over too far to the other end of the spectrum and condemning sports. Much of what I'll be calling our attention to can be enjoyed, but we must be humble enough to see the seeds of pride and self-focus.

Celebration

I remember traveling a great distance to cheer on my NFL team. One of the highlights occurred prior to the opening kickoff. It was actually when a player I greatly admired ran out of the tunnel after his name was announced. As I shared in the applause of tens of thousands, I did not even consider how prideful this moment could be.

I believe Christians can share in a moment like that and get a taste of heaven. It is truly a unifying moment that creates some unique fellowship, but Christians must be a bit discerning here. A single man was being worshiped in that moment. How does it feel for that player to run out to utter recognition and worship that rivals worship given to Christ on a Sunday? For the Christian parent, if your child is a phenomenal athlete, you must be instilling a heart of humility in her as well. Be aware of how the moments of praise on the field may be feeding a heart of pride.

To be sure, Christians can enjoy an incredible touchdown and give worship to God in the midst of the cheering fans. More often than not, though, it is celebration of creation over Creator. As the receiver points to his number and fans share conversations about him before, during, and after the Sunday morning service, we are simply participating in the praise of man and we must be more discerning.

Money

We have already spent an entire chapter discussing money, but there's a slight distinction when considering it from this perspective. When we consider the Tower of Babel account in Genesis 11, the people were all about making a name for themselves. They took the greatest resources they had – time, talent, and money – to attempt to reach the heavens. Is this not what many universities do? Money is thrown at eighteen-year-olds to create an empire. Millions upon millions are poured into coliseums that will house tens of thousands of people, with the focus of making their name known.

All the money paid to players and coaches are investments in the hopes of recognition. No program dumps money into a program to lose and be nameless. Every program wants to win because the attention follows, the program is put on the map, and recruits will come. Colleges long to win so they can boast about being the greatest. The praise of man is at the root of the money spent.

Those of you sending money to your college football programs, must search your hearts for the roots of praise that are present. For the parent who spends around $2,500 on equipment for their child to play select baseball, they must be doing some serious heart-searching.[5]

Worship

Much of what we're talking about when it comes to sports and athletes is worship. It runs through so much of what we appreciate, yet it often goes unnoticed. I want to be very cautious with the following example, but I want us to consider something.

Let's think back to the example of Travis Rudolph which I said was admirable, and it literally brought me to tears as I read it. What if we had the same example of Bo Paske sitting by himself in the cafeteria, and we replaced Rudolph with a teacher? Would it make the headlines? Would much of the country be talking about that? I don't think so.

I am moved when I hear of athletes visiting hospitals and doing charitable works. I love it when athletes use their platform for good. I am not trying to discourage that in any way and I hope we continue to see athletes leading in this way. I am trying to get us to see the worship that we've grown accustomed to. Much of what makes these moments special lies in the fact that we worship athletes. To say it another way, if we did not attribute godlike status to athletes, it would seem less special when they do these charitable works. It is often our idolatrous worship that undergirds many of these moments.

5. 'The Finances of Youth Sports in the United States.' Ohio University, https://onlinemasters.ohio.edu/the-finances-of-youth-sports-in-the-united-states/; last accessed February 2018.

Let me again stress caution here. Our Creator has given these athletes greatness. And when their greatness dwells with brokenness, it is a beautiful thing. I am not discouraging that. What I am saying is that there is idolatry in our hearts that can go unnoticed, and we must be aware it is present and all of this is simply stewardship of praise. Just as we steward all things, we must be stewarding our hearts in this specific area.

Stewarding Service and Humility

When it comes to our young children's involvement in sports, this entire issue of pride should raise concern. Scripture tells us that, 'Folly is bound up in the heart of a child ...' (Prov. 22:15a). It is the task of the parent, coach, youth pastor to instill wisdom in order to combat that folly. Therefore, we must be stewarding the next generation to that end and stewarding them in a biblical understanding of praise is a must.

We must teach our children to put others first (Luke 6:31). We must tell them that the first shall be last (Matt. 20:16), the greatest are those who serve, and that the praise of man is empty. We must warn them of the pride in their heart and how the human heart is deceitful above all else (Jer. 17:9). It is our task to teach them these things, and when so many of our sports are centered on the praise of man, we are failing if we do not try to open the eyes of our children to that reality.

When it comes to losing, as stated earlier, we must be understanding of the bitter taste of defeat. While mourning might sound like a strong word to some, I think it is appropriate. Adam and Eve knew no loss prior to sin. It is also clear that loss will be an afterthought in the new heavens and new earth; therefore, losing is unnatural. That being said, losing is part of life in a broken world and our children must steward the lack of praise associated with it. To say it this way: Christian athletes must be the best losers on earth. That is to say, they must not be sore losers. They must not be cry-babies when they lose. They must swallow the bitter tasting cup of defeat and use it to propel them to win the next time.

Again, Christian parents must steward our children in their losses, understanding that it is never fun to lose. But, much of the pain that's associated with losing lies in the fact that their prideful hearts are being assaulted. In the moments of loss, our children are getting an eternally valuable lesson in humility that they desperately need. Are you stewarding those moments or missing these opportunities?

I remember teaching Sunday school to a group of seventh and eighth graders one morning when we got on a related discussion about being Christlike in our athletics. I was telling the students that one of my favorite things to see in athletics is a player helping their opponent up off the field or some related act of sportsmanship toward their competitor. To me, it is those moments that communicate godly humility and service. It is those moments that assault the prevalence of pride that's often on the field.

To my surprise, however, many of the seventh and eighth graders protested this. Many said their parents instructed them to never help their opponents up. In essence they said their opponents were the enemy and assisting them was a form of weakness. While I was confident that many Christian families shared this sentiment, I was a bit surprised by the number of students that seemed to echo this belief.

I think this story illustrates the lack of stewardship of praise that's so prevalent in sports. Christians displaying acts of service on the field, putting others first, accepting a loss. For these students, an act of humility towards an opponent wasn't just foreign, but wrong in their minds. They were shocked I was encouraging them to assist 'the enemy' on the field of play. I wonder what they think of the words of Christ, not telling them to assist the enemy, but love them.

PART THREE
POST GAME

CHAPTER 9

THE HEART OF THE MATTER

Strap, God wants you on the floor.
— COACH NORMAN DALE, *Hoosiers* (1986)

AS we direct the focus of our stewardship to the soul of a child, I want to reflect upon some words that Dr. Walt Mueller, President of the Center for Parent/Youth Understanding, once said:

> *[Youth Culture's] rate of change is speeding up, not slowing down – and if we hesitate, stand still, and don't stay on top of the rapid changes, we'll be left in the dust ... Not only are there more voices taking up space in youth culture all the time, but they're also getting louder, more attractive, and more convincing. The question a concerned father asked me fifteen years ago rings truer every day: 'How can I expect my son to hear the still small voice of God with all those other voices screaming in his ears?'*[1]

I have served in student ministry for over a decade. Much of my adult life has been spent around teenagers. I've been immersed in their conversations. In their likes and dislikes. Their music and movies. Their fashion. Much of my time has been spent studying their culture and getting to see the world through the eyes of a teenager.

When I first started serving in youth ministry, in my college years, people saw me as the younger guy who could play with teenagers. I'm sure to those who hired me, I was simply a

---

1. Walt Mueller, *Youth Culture 101* (Youth Specialties: El Cajon, CA. 2007), p. 8.

younger Christian that could make Christianity appealing to some teens. I do not say this to criticize; I think there's some validity to that way of thinking. I knew the video games they played and there was a brief time when I could beat them at those games.

What has changed since my college years (besides my hairline and hair color), is the fact that my eyes have been opened. The young guy who simply threw the Frisbee with teenagers has been humbled by ministry. I've been humbled by my failures. By the ways I've hurt others. By the way I've been unfaithful in ministry. Now that I'm a father of five, I've been humbled to realize how hard parenting is. I realize that I don't have it figured out.

Through my years in student ministry, I've been humbled – and shocked – to see the issues students are dealing with. To be more candid, I've wept over their struggles. I've had students that have participated in all sorts of sexual sins. Sins ranging from oral sex to same-sex issues. I've had students engaged in serious drug problems. I've had students consider suicide and wrestle with eating disorders. I've lost count of students who are addicted to pornography. More than one parent has been in my office in tears over this issue.

'A sizeable percentage of young people today are delaying adulthood,' says, Denny Burk, 'In particular, they are delaying marriage and childbearing, but they are not delaying sex … The temptation is always there to suppress or revise biblical norms in order to accommodate the powerful twin influences of culture and fleshly desire.'[2] The sexual temptation teenagers of today face has been amplified and much of it is due to the influence of technology, specifically social media. It has only poured fuel on the fire of the already burning sexuality in adolescents.

The teenagers of today are dealing with weighty issues I was not equipped to deal with as I started in student ministry, and

2. Denny Burk, *What is the Meaning of Sex?* (Wheaton IL: Crossway Books, 2013), p. 217.

I struggle to keep up with how to best counsel teens dealing with new issues like the complexities surrounding the transgender movement, for example. Our teens have issues that are so big and so complex, and their weight and complexities are only intensified by the regular stressors of students' lives.

Not only are teens struggling with body image, pornography, drugs, and sexual sin; they are also struggling to keep a good grade-point average (GPA). While the background noise of their waist-line plagues them, they are trying to keep that 'A' in AP Calculus. They're depressed because they lost their starting position on the team to an underclassman, and this only adds to their thoughts of suicide.

Their struggle to make the grades, maintain a part-time job, and finish their homework only keeps their inner-struggles with sexual temptation something that stays buried. 'By the time many students reach the middle of their junior year of high school, they want (most of them say 'need') more money, and almost always that means finding a job. Research has shown that getting even a part-time job exponentially adds to the level of stress and busyness in the life of a midadolescent.'[3]

Issues are coming at our teens at 90 mph, and we've hardly touched on their spiritual lives. To be sure, every one of the above-mentioned issues is rooted in spiritual matters, but what about their devotional lives? What about their Bible reading and prayer time? What about their church attendance?

As soon as one talks about Bible reading and church attendance, the 'L-word' will most assuredly be uttered. Legalism! will be the cry of some. Please hear me say that we are *not* saved by our Bible reading or church attendance. No one is saved by their religious practices. However, those who are saved will flourish as they read the Word, and will grow as they enter community with other believers on Sundays and throughout the week. Not only will this be a desire for believers, but believers

---

3. Chap Clark, *Hurt: Inside the World of Today's Teenagers*. (Grand Rapids, MI: Baker Academic: 2004), p. 139.

will understand that they *need* God's Word speaking into their lives and they *need* fellowship with other believers to make it through this broken life.

The entire focus of this book has been on stewardship, and now we're considering the stewardship of a child's soul. The salvation of any human is in the hand of God alone. God can and will save anyone by whatever means He chooses. Nevertheless, God most often uses the Bible, parents, and pastors to bring children to salvation.[4]

Realizing that God has placed these eternal souls under our care is sobering. How are we stewarding these young souls? Can we, as parents and pastors, say that we've strived by God's grace to pass the faith along to them? Have we prayed for discipline, wisdom, and strength to teach our children God's Word?

William P. Farely gives some helpful perspective in the following statement:

> *Christians parent with one eye on eternity. Their children will live forever. This is a staggering thought. We cannot imagine 'forever.' Nevertheless, the destiny of our children either will be love that surpasses knowledge, joy inexpressible and full of glory, coupled with peace that passes understanding, or it will be weeping, wailing, and gnashing of teeth. There is no middle ground. Therefore, the Christian does not parent for this life only. The believing parent labors to prepare each child for the day of judgment. The stakes are inexpressibly high.[5]*

Now, of course, every parent is imperfect in their calling as a parent, which is part of the reason we need Jesus. There was only one perfect parent, and it's not you. However, it is quite sobering to think about giving an account of the eternal souls

---

4. William P. Farley says, 'God uses the normal means of grace to draw our children to himself. Parents are the "means" that God wants to use to reach our children. This means that we are responsible to reach our children for Christ.' *Gospel-powered Parenting: How the Gospel Shapes and Transforms Parenting* (Philipsburg, NJ: P&R Publishing, 2009), p. 21.

5. Ibid. p. 41.

that are under your care. Again, God owns these souls just like He owns our time and money, but He places them under our care to steward.

Coaching

I am often amazed by the various plays coaches and seasoned players call throughout the game. More specifically, I am amazed when the game is on the line, the clock is ticking closer to zero, and coaches are calling plays with little time for thought. And, it's obviously impressive when they do so in such a way that orchestrates a victory under those circumstances.

When coaches or players 'call a certain play,' they are implementing something every player on their team understands. They use terminology or hand signals that tell the players exactly what to do. When the play is called, everyone is on the same page and knows what's expected of them.

We must know that as parents or pastors, we know what's expected of us. God has told us in His Word what our responsibilities are. He has given us instruction. Yes, there are complexities, and we may find ourselves in a similar circumstance as the coach – which doesn't allow much time for thought or reflection – but God has clearly told us what He wants us to do. God wants His followers to make disciples.

When we read Matthew 28:18-20 it says:

> *And Jesus came and said to them, 'All authority in heaven and on earth has been given to me. Go therefore and make disciples of all nations, baptizing them in the name of the Father and of the Son and of the Holy Spirit, teaching them to observe all that I have commanded you. And behold, I am with you always, to the end of the age.*

Now, this section in Matthew is a broad call to discipleship. That is, we're told to make disciples, but this could be implemented and practiced in varying ways. It could be likened to saying that any athlete knows they are to beat their competitor; however, the way they go about beating them can be approached in many different ways. In similar fashion, discipleship takes on many shapes and sizes, but Christians are to make disciples.

In light of this call to make disciples, we also need to see that one of the earliest institutions God created was the family. Therefore, we could say that discipleship within the family is primary. Deuteronomy 6:4-9 also assists in broadening our thoughts on family. This passage calls us to see family as being broadened to the entire tribe of Israel. In the midst of this tribe, people were to be passing their faith on to the next generation. Their faith was to be 'diligently' taught 'when you sit in your house, and when you walk by the way, and when you lie down, and when you rise.' (v. 7). The discipleship of the faith communicated in Deuteronomy 6 is pretty all-encompassing.[6]

In short, it is to take place when the sun rises to the place where it sets. Teaching our children to love the Lord their God with all their heart, soul, mind, and strength is the parent's calling each and every day. James M. Hamilton Jr. says the following:

> *The call to recognize the Lord alone as God in Deuteronomy 6:4 is followed by what Jesus identified as the first and greatest*

---

6. 'Moses provided intensely practical instructions to Israelite fathers regarding *when* they were to repeat and to discuss these words: *all the time.* "When you sit in your house, and when you walk by the way, and when you lie down, and when you rise," Moses declared (v. 7). At the beginning of each day and at the end of each day, fathers were called to repeat and to discuss God's words. In between rising in the morning and lying down at night, as fathers went from place to place with their sons, they were to repeat and discuss God's words. When fathers sat in their homes with their sons, they were to repeat and discuss God's words. The first phrase of Deuteronomy 6:7 could be translated very directly as follows: "And you shall repeat them to your sons and you shall talk about them" (Although many translations change the word for "sons" to the more generic "children", the use of the Hebrew term for "sons" in this text is intentional and significant). ... The fact that the forms are masculine singular means that, as Moses addressed the nation of Israel, he directed the responsibility to teach the "sons" toward the fathers.' James M. Hamilton, 37-38, Randy Stinson and Timothy Paul Jones, *Trained in the Fear of God: Family Ministry in Theological, Historical and Practical Perspective.* (Grand Rapids, MI: Kregel Publications, 2011).

commandment: to love the Lord with all that one is and has (see Matt. 22:37-38). Heart, soul, and strength are to be exerted to exhaustion in love for the Lord. Emotions, life, and physical body powered by loving the Lord. This can be nothing less than that everything one thinks, does, and feels is to be focused on loving God.[7]

Further, seeing family in the broader context of the covenant community, it is also the job of the pastor – senior, associate, assistant, and youth. It is the job of the Sunday school teachers. It is the job of the elderly man or woman, who is too ill to make it to church to be praying for the children who are born into their church body. Passing the faith on to the next generation is paramount for believers.

It seems that many parents see the passing on of the faith as the job of the pastors and not their own. That being said, some of the blame must be laid upon the shoulders of the church. When it comes to parents failing to disciple their children, how has the church instructed the parents in this realm? '[T]he issue seems to be not so much that parents have resigned their role as primary disciple-makers,' says, Timothy Paul Jones, 'It isn't even that parents don't desire to disciple their children. In most cases, the problem is that churches are neither expecting nor equipping parents to disciple their children.'[8]

Therefore, blame is to be placed on the church, but it must also be placed on the parents. There have been two examples of this lack of seriousness to disciple children that I have seen in my time in student ministry. First, I have been shocked to discover that students don't know their parent's testimony, and parents don't know their children's testimony. This may seem like a small matter to some, but by the time I meet with students they are of junior or senior high age.

---

7. Ibid. p. 36.

8. Timothy Paul Jones, *Family Ministry Field Guide: How Your Church Can Equip Parents to Make Disciples.* (Indianapolis, IN: Wesleyan Publishing House, 2011), p. 108.

I would assume parents would talk to their children about their faith in Jesus Christ. I would assume parents would desire to evangelize their children and speak of the faith they have. Our faith has everything to do with stories. God has given us stories to make sense of the faith and communicate faith. Therefore, I am puzzled when parents are not sharing their stories with their children. There is an eternity that awaits them.

Secondly, I have also been surprised by how few parents talk to their children about sex. One time I was meeting with a small group of senior high guys, and they all gave testimony to this fact. They said that their fathers might have had one talk with them or the father shared part of a talk with them but was too embarrassed to go on. Most, however, said their fathers never spoke with them about sex. Please know, these are great guys from great families, but they weren't having these discussions.

Paul David Tripp relays this sentiment when he said: 'Christian parents don't seem to do a very good job in discipling their children in [this] area. How many parents do more than have one creepy, quasi-embarrassed talk about sex, with joy once it's over and a determination never to talk about it again?'[9]

Think of the plethora of sexual-related issues in our culture: fornication, homosexuality, and transgenderism, just to name a few. The young men in my youth group were moving to college in a matter of years without a biblical framework of sex and sexuality. The biblical worldview these parents were responsible for passing on to their children was not communicated. These young men were unarmed as they moved out into a culture that is denying the sexual ethic of Scripture. I was in disbelief.

While there are families that diligently strive to pass the faith on, it seems that many families are not. It seems that busyness is a major contributing factor and sports would be a contributing factor to that busyness.

---

9. Paul David Tripp, *Sex and Money: Pleasures that Leave You Empty and Grace that Satisfies* (Wheaton, IL: Crossway Books, 2013), p. 17.

For a significant minority of parents, it was children's sports and school activities that trumped family time when it came to scheduling priorities. Nearly one-third of parents agreed that they were willing, at some level, 'to do whatever it takes' for their children to succeed in certain sports or school activities. And what if the resulting schedule was so hectic that it prevented the family from eating any meals together during the week? As long as the payoff at the end included academic or athletic success for their child, these parents were willing to pay the price.[10]

The commitment to youth sports is so all-consuming that it leaves little to no time to discuss the faith, not only the essential truth of what faith is or what repentance is, but specific matters like sex as well. The Christian community has become so enamored with youth sports and gives so much time, money and energy to them, that we have lost perspective on the souls that are out on the field.

Since we place so much value in sports – because of the time and money associated with them – sports have become primary in our mind. While any Christian parent would say that the faith of the child is primary, our practices in the Christian community seem to be illustrating the very opposite. Let me give you another example.

Most churches have some sort of class or process for young children seeking to become a member of their church. I know this varies from context to context, but there is some sort of 'new members' class church-goers are familiar with. While these classes may vary, there are many of them that meet on Sundays during a Sunday school hour, the evening, or even in the afternoon.

We also know that many sports leagues/teams host tournaments or practices during Sundays. The reality is, the two – church membership and team membership – are going to collide. Most of us are also aware of which group will receive membership during that specific day.

---

10. Timothy Paul Jones, *Family Ministry Field Guide*, p. 101.

But, let's stop and consider the two meetings.

The team membership builds character, physical strength, and relationships among the team – all very important and biblical things. The church membership, in most cases, has students asking these questions: Do I believe in God? What does it mean to place my faith in Jesus Christ? Who is Jesus? What is sin?

Both of the above are good and biblical, but one is dealing with ultimate questions and the other is dealing with secondary matters. To be sure, the team membership can add richness and deeper understanding to the ultimate questions, but the ultimate questions must be dealt first.

To put it bluntly, our Christianity is far more important than our sport. Our Christianity informs how we are a teammate. Our Christianity shapes the way we handle a loss or the way we celebrate a win. Our Christianity influences our understanding of physical strength and endurance. Our Christianity will be around long after the sport we play. And, if everything was laid to the side for our sport – including the church – what are the chances of these young students picking church up later in life?

In the call to steward the faith of our children, we must think about how they are interpreting life around them. When hours and hours and hours are given to a sport and dollars upon dollars upon dollars are being spent on a sport, what message is that sending a child? They clearly learn what is important. When the sharing of our faith, the joining of a church, the talks on biblical sexuality have ceased to take place in a *Christian* home (!), what kind of faith is being passed on? How will we, as parents and pastors, answer to God about discipling the next generation?

John Piper once addressed a group of youth pastors in a talk entitled, *Imparting A Passion: A Challenge to Youth Workers*. In that address he said the following:

> *I want to begin by asking you a question that comes from the book of Acts. When your present generation of student graduates will you be able to say what the Apostle Paul says in Acts 20:26, 'I testify to*

you this day that I am innocent of the blood of all of you. For I did not shrink from declaring to you the whole counsel of God.' I did not shrink from declaring to you, young people, the counsel of God. I am innocent of your blood as you graduate from high school.

Have you even set a tone where a statement like that could even be heard with any seriousness? Would that sound so strange coming out of your mouth? I am innocent of your blood, young people. Would that sound so strange to them, given the way you've ministered to them that you would even dare to say such a thing because it would sound so screwy in their heads… your blood is not on my hands … this true faith does not come from singing, it comes from the truth we sing. You can get hands up in the air in a second, from the right crescendo, but what about when they suffer? What about when they're rejected? Will they embrace [truth]? Will they burn for Christ when there are no notes playing, no CDs, nobody else around? Just rejection. Just suffering. Just sickness. Will they burn? That's the only kind of young people we want to breed.[11]

I remember hearing this message years ago and being so impacted by it. The Lord has used the message over and over again in my years of the ministry to continue to call me to the truth of being 'innocent of the blood' of my students. I am confident that I have failed in this call, because I am confident I am a sinner. I am also confident that by God's grace alone I have sought to teach God's Word faithfully to my students and impart a passionate faith to the next generation.

To be sure, there are times I have not emphasized grace enough. There are times I have not emphasized holiness enough. There are times when I have been unloving, unkind, impatient, and hurtful with my words towards students and families. I have gossiped about them. I have missed opportunities to share the gospel and serve alongside them. Nevertheless, I know I have kept the Word before them, and God has graciously shown me the need to impart the faith to the next generation.

---

11. John Piper, *Imparting a Passion: A Challenge to Youth Workers*. Desiring God. http://www.desiringgod.org/messages/imparting-a-passion-a-challenge -to-youth-workers; last accessed February 2018.

Let me direct this challenge at the mothers and fathers reading this, how are you stewarding your child's eternal soul? Pastor or spiritual parent, how are you discipling students in your care? Coach, are you allowing your players to be in church on Sundays and allowing them time for Bible studies during the week? Yes, our children can learn so many valuable lessons on the field, but there is absolutely no substitute for God's Word.

Let me go a step further to say that a sideline devotional on a Sunday does not suffice for God's worship. A coach who thinks a sideline devotional is what God intended for His worship on His day makes me fearful to think what that coach would be communicating from God's Word. If he truly thinks a pregame devotional is God-honoring, it makes me fearful to think how he or she interprets the rest of God's Word. But, what gives me greater concern is the young heart and mind that's listening and being influenced by that example.

CHAPTER 10

OFF THE FIELD: THE BROADER SPORTS CULTURE

Ballplayers. I don't have ballplayers, I've got girls.
—JIMMY DUGAN, *A League of Their Own* (1992)

BEFORE we conclude discussion on the stewardship of sports, there's one more important aspect to consider. While this chapter doesn't explicitly deal with a stewardship issue, it gets us to think about the broader culture sports occur in. To put it another way, youth sports don't occur in a vacuum. Youth sports are a part of the culture and there are major cultural issues Christians should be thinking about. More specifically, there are some alarming cultural trends occurring and we, as Christian parents, must be preparing our youth for some of the cultural trends their generation will be dealing with.

R. Albert Mohler, Jr., President of the Southern Baptist Theological Seminary, says, 'Today's generation often encounters material that no previous generation could possibly have comprehended.'[1] To further illustrate this axiom, he explains that some pre-schools in European countries prohibit the use of gendered pronouns[2] and others are seeking to deny the 'objective reality of gender altogether.'[3]

---

1. R. Albert Mohler, Jr., *We Cannot Be Silent: Speaking Truth to a Culture Redefining Sex, Marriage, and the Very Meaning of Right and Wrong* (Nashville: Thomas Nelson, 2015), p. 81.

2. Ibid., p. 84.

3. Ibid., p. 87.

Many in the church today aren't even awake to the realities of the transgender movement, while some church leaders are seeking wisdom from God's Word on how to minister to a Lesbian Gay Bisexual Transgender (LGBT) culture. There are, no doubt, some pastors seeking to understand the LGBT movement. However, the culture has already moved on to acronyms like QUILTBAG – 'Queer/Questioning, Undecided, Intersex, Lesbian, Transgender/Transsexual, Bisexual, Allied/Asexual, Gay/Genderqueer'[4] – in order to more accurately describe their 'understanding' of sexuality.

The vast majority of Christians that are confronted with issues like this often react in one of two ways. First, they simply roll their eyes, and with a shake of the head dismiss what they're hearing as nonsense, as if ignoring this reality will prevent it from happening. Secondly, there are those Christians who simply think the reality of what is taking place is something 'out there' that will never find its way into the confines of their local Christian context. 'Out there' is obviously California or New York for those rural-minded Christians.

The truth is, issues surrounding the transgender movement are on many college campuses all across the world[5]. Mohler is wise to say:

> What happens on the American college and university campus never stays there, nor is it intended to … [it] will ultimately trickle down to local high schools, kindergartens, and preschools. Ultimately, they may become the only acceptable mode of discourse in the public square. … In due time, extremely specific and difficult questions will arrive at the doorstep of **every** congregation.[6]

---

4. Ibid., p. 94.

5. While I bring up the 'issue' of transgenderism, I think it is important to be reminded that this isn't simply an 'issue' but something affecting individuals; image-bearers who are dealing with complex confusions over gender. Vaughan Roberts gave me this perspective in his helpful book, *Transgender* (The Good Book Company, 2016)

6. Ibid. pp. 95-96, 98, emphasis added.

I've just quoted from Mohler's book *We Cannot Be Silent.* I wonder if his work would have been more aptly entitled, *We Cannot Remain Asleep?* As I've said, the broader Christian culture hardly gives a passing thought to many of these issues, but those who are thinking about engaging in issues like same-sex marriage are already behind. While the church is thinking about those issues, the culture has left them in the dust. As one of my professors shared in a recent lecture, the church will be dealing with issues like bestiality and pedophilia in the next five years or less.

Sports and Culture

Why do I mention all of this? Well, our sports fit into a specific context. The culture of sports is dramatically shaped by the culture around us. For example, the former San Francisco 49ers quarterback, Colin Kaepernick, made the decision to remain seated during the singing of the national anthem. That took place in a microcosm of our culture at a football game in a stadium of approximately 70,000 people, but was shaped by the broader culture of the United States – reaching people who didn't even know anything about football or who Kapernick was, for that matter.

A football player sitting (or taking a knee) during the singing of our nation's anthem would have been unthinkable to previous generations. Even though it leaves many in our culture puzzled, there are some who understand the point Kapernick is trying to make – regardless of agreeing or disagreeing. Now, I do not bring Kapernick up to debate whether or not he is correct or incorrect. My point is, his actions are shaped by the culture around him.

Similarly, youth sports are shaped by a broader culture around them. What we have been seeing for quite some time is the culture of professional and college sports filtering down into youth sports. From end zone celebrations, jargon, accessories, attire, celebrity, and expectations, the broader sports context has shaped the climate of youth sports. It has even been reported that high schoolers are following in Kapernick's footsteps.[7]

It is that broader context many parents need to wake up to. What follows are several aspects of the culture Christians must make themselves aware of.

Technology and Pornography

Many, many years ago a student in my youth group wanted to show me a funny video on YouTube. The student attended the Christian school that was part of the church I ministered in, so he came by my office after school was over. The interchange went something like this:

> **Student**: 'You have to see this video on YouTube! It's hilarious!'
>
> **Me**: 'Sorry man. YouTube is blocked here to protect students from inappropriate content.'
>
> **Student**: [typing on my keyboard] 'All you do is type this in and you can get around the firewall ... Here it is.'

This kid was twelve years old, and in a matter of seconds he was able to bypass the security system the school was spending money on to protect young minds from inappropriate content. He informed me that students do this all the time, and teachers were completely unaware. I don't think I was even able to focus on the video he showed because I was still in shock at the ease over which he bypassed something we believed would protect him. Something I was ignorant to.

Full disclosure: I am not the most tech-savvy guy on the planet. I try to study up on technology and know something about it. One truth I have learned about technology through

---

7. It is reported that this is taking place across the United States in multiple sports platforms. CNN Wire, 'High School Football Players Join Colin Kaepernick's Movement, Creating Tensions in Player's Hometown,' September 18, 2016, http://ktla.com/2016/09/18/high-school-football-players-join-colin-kaepernicks-movement-creating-tensions-in-players-hometown; last accessed February 2018.

the years is that it's always changing, and students are typically a step or two (or three) ahead of the parents.

What is alarming is the fact that many parents do not seek to understand the technology they place in their child's hands. They don't know what capabilities a smartphone or tablet has, but that doesn't keep them from purchasing one and giving their child unlimited access to it.

Again, this goes back to a stewardship issue. Parents fail at the stewardship of their child's soul when they give them a piece of equipment they know little to nothing about. Most often, parents simply place these devices in the hands of their child in order to buy some moments of peace in the home. Parenting is exceedingly hard at times, but these devices distract long enough to keep siblings from fighting, allow parents to talk with a friend, or for parents, themselves, to check their Facebook or Instagram.

Not only are there numerous studies demonstrating the dangers of too much screen time for children,[8] but there are numerous evils lurking just a few clicks away – evils many young minds are naïve about. Pornography is one of those chief evils.

Blogger and author Tim Challies notes the differences in access to porn through the years.[9] As he says, pornography was formerly behind the counter at a gas station. Someone had to go through the embarrassment of asking for it. Now, however, pornography comes looking for you. You don't even have to be looking for it. In fact, studies show that first-time exposure to pornography for children is often accidental.

It is accidental in the sense that children unknowingly click on it. For example, perhaps a parent has given their child

---

8. The negatives range from vision impairment, sleep deprivation, and obesity to issues like anxiety and lack of social skills. Shelly Turkle has spent a considerable amount of research in a trilogy of books looking at the effects of technology on our lives: *Alone Together (2012)*, *The Second Self (2005)*, *& Life on the Screen (1997)*.

9. Tim Challies, *Sexual Detox: For Guys Who are Sick of Porn* (Adelphi, ST: Cruciform, 2010), pp. 9-10.

access to their smartphone to play a game. Many pornography companies pay for ads on those games, but they may have a secondary site that isn't explicitly pornographic. While the child is playing an 'innocent' game, they click on an ad that pops up. The ad takes them to a site, which is ultimately a gateway to pornographic material.

A second accidental form of pornography exposure for children occurs when a child hears a term from friends they are unfamiliar with. Let's use the word 'sex' for example. This particular child hears the word 'sex' from their friends on the playground, and they don't have a clue what the word means. It is obvious everyone else in the conversation knows what the word means, so they don't want to speak up and say anything. Later, when they get home, they go to Google for the answer. You can imagine what sort of images pop up on Google when the word 'sex' is typed into the search bar.

The sad reality of this second example is the fact that a child did not feel comfortable enough to ask their parent. Not only did the parent fail to educate them on what these terms are, they have not fostered a relationship where this sort of discussion can take place.

While many parents may feel that eight to ten-year-olds have no business hearing what sex is, these are the ages children are exposed to pornography. Younger and younger minds are being poisoned with pornographic material that will forever shape them. Instead of hearing that God created sex as a good thing, they are seeing satanic distortions of it first.

Serving on the frontlines of the youth culture for the past decade, I can assure you that the prevalence of pornography addiction amongst our teens is catastrophic. What's alarming to me is the fact that I have three daughters. Will they fall in love with men that have poisoned their minds with pornography for a decade? This is not to say that a husband is rendered worthless once he is exposed to pornography. What I am saying however, is that if I had a choice I would rather my daughters marry a man (if God intends for them to marry) who has had little, to no, pornography exposure.

The prevalence of pornography has become so great that we often consider it unthinkable that a man[10] can make it through his pre-teen and teenage years without succumbing to the temptations of pornography. It seems that pornography exposure has become a rite of passage or a part of life our culture should accept. Far too many parents have shrugged their shoulders in defeat over this issue. Or, maybe they view it as a means of education, an education they are too embarrassed to provide.

Homosexuality and Transgenderism

Training takes place prior to any profession. That is, before one becomes a doctor, they go to school to prepare for that. Before a lawyer goes to trial, they go to law school. In most cases, everyone feels a little ill-prepared by the time they face the real thing. Even if they had superior training, actually doing something for the first time is nerve-wracking. At least, that was the case for me as I tried to communicate my love and care for a student who came out as gay.

I had gone to seminary. I had sat in many classes that taught me many things about the Bible and how to properly use the Bible in a helpful way. However, I was unprepared to look an individual in the eyes and tell them I love them, but that I disagree with them. All the training had not given me the eloquence, wisdom, grace, and conviction I needed for that day.

I was nervous. I was confused. I was sad. I was hurting. I knew what I believed, but was put to the test in that moment. Did I really believe what I was saying? Am I right? Have I misunderstood the truth?

The testing of one's faith comes in various shapes and sizes and a conversation with a student claiming to be homosexual sure put my faith against the ropes. It is one thing to imagine scenarios where this may occur and discuss hypotheticals and quite another to have a living and breathing example right in front of you.

---

10. I know that pornography addiction is also growing among females. This issue is not simply a male issue.

If our current culture of sexual ethics has taught us anything, it is that we are to accommodate, accept, tolerate, and trumpet homosexual and transgender rights. Not only are Christians, in many contexts, unable to express the sexual ethic of Scripture, they are being forced to embrace the sexual ethic of our culture. What is more, many of our Christian students are growing more accepting of this culture than that of Scripture.

Speaking as one who is around teenagers quite often, many of our teens see the Christian teaching on homosexuality as something outdated and ill-informed. To say it another way, they disagree with the Bible's teaching on the subject. Not because they haven't been taught otherwise, but because they are taught – early and often – by the culture.

Our students are astute pupils of Lady Gaga, Kanye West, Hollywood, MTV, YouTube, and a culture that is extremely averse to God's Word. Young minds are being shaped by a culture that never stops talking about sexual perversion but not being shaped by God's teaching on the matter because parents aren't picking up the Bible in the home and teaching from it.

Pews are empty and Sunday school classrooms are missing the young minds that must be steeped in the Scriptures in order to be able to stand against a culture that is growing more hostile to Christianity. While the broader culture is making great strides to educate young minds with these new sexual ethics, Christians are treating Christian institutions and Christian doctrine as something extra. Sunday morning worship and biblical teaching in the home has now been replaced by what was once referred to as *extra*curricular activities, like sports.

Serious sexual issues like pornography, homosexuality, and transgenderism are being instilled in this younger generation, but there is little being done to combat it because there's no time to do so. While our children are becoming more sympathetic to the truisms of our culture, they are becoming less so towards biblical Christianity. Christianity is becoming something more foreign and less appealing.

Stress, Depression and Suicide

Our youth ministry has weekly prayer breakfasts with our students. Part of our design for these breakfasts is to model the importance of starting the day in God's Word and prayer. While that is part of our aim, a breakfast is becoming one of the only times we can meet with students because of their harried schedules. Even then, there are many students who can't make a breakfast either. To be sure, there are simply those students who need to sleep in a bit because of the pressures of school, but there are also those who can't make breakfast because they have school-related activities during the breakfast hour.

At one particular breakfast, I noticed that the eyelids of our students were a bit heavier than usual (it obviously wasn't a result of my teaching). I can't remember if we were about to read Scripture or pray, but I interrupted whatever it was we were doing and said something like, 'Are you guys ok? You seem a bit tired.'

The response from the students was interesting. The question seemed to perk them up a bit as they all seemed to have freedom to discuss how tired and stressed they were. This led me to ask a question about their bedtime. Midnight seemed to be the consensus of the group. Five hours of sleep seemed to be the duration of most. Some of them had late nights after sports practice. Others binge-watched Netflix. The early mornings were due to finishing projects.

The vast majority of our students are stressed to the max. Early mornings, late nights, weightlifting before school, practice every day after school, part-time jobs, scholarship opportunities, GPA, resume building, reputation, parent's expectations, acne, body image, eating disorders, ADD, medication, drug abuse, drinking, learning to drive, numerous insecurities, puberty, divorce, and social media like Instagram and Snapchat are like fuel on an already-burning fire of the teenage years.

Jean Twenge, in her book *iGen*, says, '[This generation] is on the verge of the most severe mental health crisis for young people in decades.'[11] As Twenge lays out the numerous mental health issues that are steadily increasing among this generation's teens, she draws an interesting (and not surprising) correlation: 'The sudden, sharp rise in depressive symptoms occurred at almost exactly the same time that smartphones became ubiquitous and in-person interaction plummeted.'[12]

To be very candid, and possibly a bit crass, I'm surprised the rate of teen suicide isn't higher than it already is. Our young students have a weight upon their shoulders that was unconscionable to previous generations. To be sure, those in biblical times, or frontier life, and those growing up in the Great Depression might raise their hands in protest, but the times our students are growing up in – as affluent as they are – have ushered in unique struggles that are equally depressing.

While children growing up in Rome might have seen temple prostitutes, children today are getting private lap-dances in their bedroom through Snapcash.[13] While the Great Depression rendered families so poverty stricken they often went without meals, our generation has so much excess they are able to obtain drugs to numb their insecurities.

The Notorious B.I.G. was right when he sang long ago, 'Mo money, mo problems.'[14] Even though many families today are among the richest society has ever seen, it has only added to the complexities of problems long ago. Our students are stressed by the affluence they have and are only adding to their stress in pursuit of more affluence.

Money is the driving factor behind much of our students' stress. Students are trying out for multiple sports teams in

11. Dr. Jean M. Twenge, *iGen: Why Today's Super-Connected Kids Are Growing Up Less Rebellious, More Tolerant, Less Happy – And Completely Unprepared for Adulthood – And What that Means for the Rest of Us.* (Atria Books, 2017) Kindle edition.

12. Ibid. Kindle edition.

13. Snapcash is associated with the popular social media platform, Snapchat.

14. Notorious B.I.G. (featuring Mace and Puff Daddy) *Mo Money, Mo Problems.* (1997).

order to get scholarships. Or, they are focusing on one sport and having private lessons in pursuit of that sport in order to get a scholarship. On top of that, they are studying hard to get a scholarship.

Church and church-related matters are often sidelined because those don't offer scholarships. However, church involvement still sounds good on a resume so they are sure to list it among other things, even when the students hardly darkened the doors of the church.

While busyness may be the title of our current culture, stress, worry and anxiety are accurate subheadings. Our students are dealing with so much, but don't have the time to deal with it properly. Therefore, they are simply rushed down the stream of their high school experience trying to figure it out as they go.

The point is, youth sports must be considered in that context. Context is key. For example, if I told you that one time I hit my daughter's hand as hard as I could, that would be alarming to you – rightly so. However, if I told you that my daughter's tiny fingers were within inches of a burning-orange eye on the stove, you would understand the context. The context justifies the slapping of my daughter's hand.

Likewise, the youth sports culture fits into the broader culture of our society and that society is one that has a growing disdain for Christendom. Ours is a culture that's witnessing increased persecution of Christians. Ours is a culture that has already redefined one of the most basic institutions of mankind – marriage. Ours is a culture that is redefining the word 'parent.'[15] Ours is a culture that is forcing Christians to pay for the murder of infants in the womb and moving towards practices most cultures see as barbaric when it comes to abortion. Ours is a culture that has fined Christians for asserting what they believe to be true about biblical sexuality. Ours is a culture that's threatening pastors' pulpit rhetoric.

---

15. Alan Feuer, 'New York's Highest Court Expands Definition of Parenthood,' August 30, 2016, *New York Times*.

Ours is a culture that's fueling a secularism that is intolerant of biblical Christianity, and 'Christians' are adding logs to the fire by shirking their responsibility to open God's Word to their children. Christians don't have time to deal with issues like homosexuality because they work until 6 p.m. and have to get little Johnny to practice by 6.30 p.m. They don't have time to learn about the latest app their child just downloaded on the phone in the backseat on the way to the field.

I do not seek to be an alarmist, but it is concerning to note the trends in Christianity that seem to be feeding the growing secularism. That being said, Christians must be confident in a sovereign God who is reigning and ruling. We must be confident that God has His children in His hands and no one can snatch them out (John 10:28-30). We must be confident that God has promised that the gates of hell will not overthrow His Kingdom (Matt. 16:18).

While I hope this chapter sobers many Christians to the real issues facing Christendom today, I do not want it to create an unhealthy fear in the church. We serve a Heavenly Father that constantly reminds us that He is always with us and will never leave us (Deut. 31:6). Even though the culture seems to be changing each hour, we can stand firm on that unshakable foundation.

CHAPTER 11

RULES OF ENGAGEMENT

I have to believe that when things are bad I can change them.
— JAMES J. BRADDOCK, *Cinderella Man* (2005)

I REMEMBER the greatest team I was ever a part of had two coaches that were the perfect 'Good Cop/Bad Cop' pair any team could have. They were both very skilled and hugely respected, but would go about coaching in different ways. To be fair, part of the reason the 'bad cop' earned his reputation was from all of the sprints and running he would make us do. Not only would we have to run for punishment, we would also have to run about thirty to forty-five minutes at the end of every practice.

That being said, we dominated teams that year. We were very successful and a great deal of that success was due in part to all the running. You see, in the second half of almost every game our opponents would be fatigued, understandably. We, however, would not be. It really seemed like we would run circles around most teams, because we had focused so much on endurance.

To use the language that's the focus of this book, the coach had *stewarded* his players well. He had spent hour upon hour preparing us for the second half and that stewardship paid off with multiple convincing victories.

Well, we are reaching the conclusion of this book and I trust you see the importance of stewardship. Whether we like it or not, we are God's stewards. God has clearly given humanity stewardship of His creation – money, time, identities, bodies, humility, and souls are included in this call of faithful stewardship.

Of course, our calling as God's stewards is under attack by Satan. To say it another way, if God calls us to this task, Satan's task will be to frustrate it. What the aforementioned has shown is how gradually over time, Satan has caused us to lose sight of this job as stewards and has led to a misuse – and in some cases abuse – of the gifts God has given us.

If you've made it this far in the book, perhaps you fit into one of the following categories. First, maybe you are someone who loves sports to such a degree that you deplore much of what I've said. Therefore, you're only continuing to read in order to refute any argument I'm making about sports stewardship. If you fall into this category, I sincerely applaud you for making it this far and for your willingness to listen to what I have to say. Maybe we could have a loving discussion sometime on this?

You may fall into a second category. Maybe you hate sports and, instead of deploring much of what I've said, you applaud it to such a degree that it fuels your dislike. Even though I agree that there is much to critique in the sports culture and much I think the church should be more discerning about, I also think it's important to have Christians in the sports culture. Not only do we need to be in the world as Christians, we also need to see sports as a gracious gift from God that Christians can participate in.

While there are plenty of possible categories, maybe you fall into a third one. Perhaps you are a Christian who loves God and loves sports. Perhaps you seek to love the Lord your God with all your heart, soul, mind, and strength. You love your church; you try to read the Bible and apply it to life. You sincerely love Jesus, and you wonder what sort of an impact that should have on sports. Maybe God has blessed you with children that are gifted athletically, and you wonder how they could be used in this sphere of God's creation.

If you are in this last category, this is who I wrote the book for. If you are in this last category, I'm in it with you. Now that you've made it this far, I guess I could be a bit vulnerable and say that I wrote much of this for … me. I know, I'm selfish.

You see, I'm a fellow pilgrim with you who's trying to figure out how to discerningly live this life prior to going home. I see so much to be concerned about in the youth sports culture. At the same time, I want my own children to be involved in sports. I want them to be athletic. I want them to play various sports and to play them well. But, more than that, I want them to love Jesus and treasure Him more than anything else.

I say that knowing that it doesn't have to be an either or. I know my children can love Jesus *and* play sports. I know they can love Jesus *while* playing sports. I know they can love Jesus and *display that through* playing sports. The truth is however, I must ensure I'm spending a great deal of time and prayer telling them about Jesus so they'll want to play in a way that displays His love.

In this chapter, I will attempt to lay down some guidelines and boundaries for Christian families seeking to be a part of the youth sports culture. I'm seeking to use Scripture as my guide in these assertions, and it is my prayer that they help, but there's one problem in all of this: sin. Mine and yours.

Sin clouds my mind and my thinking and my heart; it does so to you as well. Therefore, we approach God's Word as sinners who do not fully grasp God's Word and love it as we should. Our sin not only clouds our thinking of God's Word, it also clouds our thinking on sports. Our sin turns a good thing, like sports, into an idol. It justifies certain thoughts and practices we take up that are less than good. Our sin makes things difficult, to say the least.

Let me go ahead and warn you that some of what I assert may seem ridiculous to you. Even though you may shake your head in disagreement, I think much of what has become normative in our youth sports culture is ridiculous. You see, I think many Christians have jumped into the youth sports culture with little discernment. Out of this lack of discernment, we've come to accept rituals and practices that may have been unthinkable to previous generations.

While some of what's to follow may seem extreme, know that I have sought to keep God's Word at the foundation of all I assert. Taking into account my own sin and finiteness, I've sought to have the Word shine through the clouds of confusion. It is my earnest prayer that what follows assists many Christian families in their engagement of sports, and that by implementing these practices, families are able to further enjoy sports and glorify God through them.

Keep the Main Thing, the Main Thing

Every sport has fundamentals. Fundamentals are basic skills an athlete must learn before they can succeed. They must have these fundamentals ingrained in their psyche in order to properly execute on the field. If this foundation is not present, there will be a collapse in the athlete. Foundations are vital for stability.

I get the sense that much of the sports culture begins so early and begins with such intensity that Christian families are rushing past fundamentals – fundamentals of the Christian faith, that is. While anyone is saved by grace alone, through faith alone, in Christ alone, Christian parents must take great Spirit-filled strides to instill a solid biblical foundation in their children. However, it takes time to build this foundation, and it is that required time that seems to be absent from many families.

At a very early age, I professed faith in Jesus Christ. But I will be the first to tell you that my grasp of that faith was miniscule (not that we can ever fully grasp it this side of heaven). While I would also be the first to affirm the Scripture's emphasis of a mustard-seed-like-faith, I didn't really understand what I was professing, so much so that I've actually wondered if it wasn't until later in life that I was converted.

In the matter of our children's salvation, little (nothing) else is higher priority. Christian parents are charged throughout Scripture to pass the faith along to the next generation. As already illustrated from Deuteronomy 6 and Matthew 28, parents should be aware that this disciple-making begins in the home.

With the command to love God with all our heart, soul, mind and strength and to pass that on, Christians should be unanimous in their understanding of this importance. In other words, it should be a basic fundamental of the Christian faith, a fundamental we are teaching our children. Truth be told however, the frequency and intensity of youth-related sports doesn't leave much time for these fundamentals.

The only 'answer' I can give will come across as simplistic to many, but you must keep the main thing the main thing. For Christians to love the Lord above all else, they must keep the Lord above all else. Parents must seek to keep their children in church and open up the Word in the home. This is simply a must. If sports are interfering with this, then cut back on sports. It's simple but true.

This does not mean that your child has to drop off of the team, but maybe it means leaving practice early in order to get to church or get home to have a time of devotion with the family. God entrusts children to parents, not coaches. While coaches are very important in the development of a child, they will not give an account to the Lord for how they raised *your* child. God entrusts young souls to their parents and their parents are to 'diligently' impress this faith upon them.

We must get even more fundamental than this, however. Parents must have time to personally connect with the Lover of their souls. Even more fundamental than parents passing the faith on is a parent stewarding their own faith so that they have a faith to pass on. Parents must keep God first in their life, and they cannot do this well if they aren't taking the time to do it.

As Christians, we are united to Jesus Christ and nothing can take that glorious truth away. Kevin DeYoung, however, gives some helpful thoughts on the difference between union and communion:

> *Nothing can make us a little more or a little less united [with Christ]. Union with Christ is unalterable. Communion with Christ, on the other hand, can be affected by sin and unresponsive to God's grace. It's like marriage: you can't be more or less married (union) but you can have a stronger or weaker marriage (communion). Our relationship can also deepen when we attend to the divinely appointed means of grace. Or to put it somewhat paradoxically, we*

who enjoy saving fellowship in Christ ought to cultivate a growing fellowship with Christ.[1]

While the implementation of this first truth can be discussed and debated, the truth itself cannot. Any Christian knows that their relationship with the Lord takes priority above *all* else. Parents must guard their own faith and the faith they pass on to their children. If sports is hindering this, then Christians must do whatever it takes to fight for their faith. Simply stated, faith is more important than sports. If one is impeding the other, one of them has to go and there's only one right answer.

Leave and Cleave

Christians are growing up in a culture that detests the biblical definition of marriage.[2] We live in a culture that has redefined this centuries-old institution, and it appears that a younger generation of 'Christians' are buying into this new definition. Since the culture is growing ever more hostile to the Bible's understanding

---

1. Kevin DeYoung, *The Hole in Our Holiness: Filling the Gap between Gospel Passion and the Pursuit of Godliness.* (Wheaton, IL: Crossway Books, 2012), p. 124.

2. Jean Twenge, *iGen: Why Today's Super-Connected Kids Are Growing Up Less Rebellious, More Tolerant, Less Happy-and Completely Unprepared for Adulthood-and What That Means for the Rest of Us.* 'When the Supreme Court ruled in June 2015 that same-sex marriage was legal nationwide, Snickers tweeted a picture of a rainbow-wrapped candy bar inscribed "Stay who you are". AT&T turned its globe logo to rainbow hues, and American Airlines tweeted, "We're on board. Diversity strengthens us all and today we celebrate #MarriageEquality". It's rare for companies to chime in on social issues, as they'd rather not alienate their customers. For a company like American, headquarters in Texas, that could be a lot of customers. But American and other companies are looking toward an *iGen* future, seeking to appeal to the young consumers who will fuel their bottom line in years to come. Companies know that embracing equality is not just an expectation for *iGen*; it's a requirement.' Twenge points out that 64 per cent think Christianity is antigay, 62 per cent think it's judgmental, and 58 per cent think it's hypocritical. She quotes a student who says, 'I'm religious and love God, but the rules are too strict. And some of them are prejudicial, like not liking homosexuality ... I think people don't want to live with that kind of thinking anymore. It's a disgusting way to treat other people.' Kindle edition.

of marriage, Christians must understand that they will be required to fight for this God-ordained institution. As John Piper says, 'The fact that we live in a society that can defend two men or two women entering a sexual relationship and, with wild inconceivability, call it *marriage* shows that the collapse of our culture into debauchery and anarchy is probably not far away.'[3]

Given the biblical importance of marriage and the primacy it is to have over any earthly relationship, Christians must be cautious of how this culture will seek to minimize marriage. In light of that, I think there is a subtle way in which marriage has been undermined, and this subtlety has occurred through one of the gifts of marriage itself; procreation.

To put it candidly, spouses come before children. 'Too often as husbands and wives we seek our completeness in other things – our job, our children, our hobbies,' says, Tim Savage, 'But in marriage we are called to find our completeness in the sacrificial nurture of our partner. We must be wise enough to recognize this calling and humble enough to embrace it. We must confess our need, not in the first instance to receive from, but to give to our partner.'[4]

Marriage is a beautiful thing, but good marriages take work. Work, however, takes time. Extra time, however, seems to be lacking from many Christian's schedules.

God is to be first in every human's life. For those who are married, their spouse comes second. Children need to know how much their parents love and support them, to know they are safe and can talk to them about anything, but they also need to know they come in second to Mommy or Daddy. That may sound harsh to some, but it is one of the most loving things you can teach your children. More importantly the Bible says so. It clearly says, 'a man is to leave his father and mother and hold fast to his wife' (Gen. 2:24). This is giving priority to the marriage relationship.

---

3. John Piper, *This Momentary Marriage: A Parable of Permanence*. (Wheaton, IL: Crossway Books, 2009), p. 20.

4. Tim Savage, *No Ordinary Marriage: Together for God's Glory*. (Wheaton, IL: Crossway Books, 2012), p. 41.

I have heard countless parents talk about never missing their child's game, and I had two of the most loving parents that never missed my games. That is admirable, and parents should be commended for their love and support of their children, but maybe they should miss a few games from time to time?

There is no doubt that husbands and wives can strengthen their marriages in the stands as they cheer on little Johnny, but maybe they should go on a date and have a real conversation? You see, when husbands and wives are cheering on their child, their child is the focus ... not the marriage. It would do the child some good to have their parents miss a game in order to remind them they are not the center of the universe. Maybe couples don't have to miss a game to make this happen, but I believe that most families don't have much free time in their schedules.

Husbands and wives must have consistent time together to build a strong marriage. I heard someone say one time that communication is the life-blood of the marriage. Wayne Mack says, 'Deep oneness can be achieved only where good communication exists ... No two people can effectively walk together, work together, or live together without a good communications system.'[5] You cannot have a good marriage if there's no communication. Just as any Christian needs communication with God through prayer and the Word to have a relationship with Him, husbands and wives must have communication.

If you Google information on couples spending time together, you will find studies saying that the average couples spend anywhere from fifteen to thirty minutes together in a given week. That's a recipe for disaster. While it might sound shocking, it doesn't sound inaccurate.

Truth be told, many husbands and wives are living like roommates with each other. One of the major contributing factors is a child-centered home. These couples have spent so

---

5. Wayne Mack, *Strengthening Your Marriage*. (Phillipsburg, NJ: P&R Publishing, 1999), p. 55.

much time focusing on the children that there isn't much left for the two of them. Perhaps this has gotten to such an extreme that these couples are only staying together because of the children. Maybe the divided home that exists because of sports is by design and necessity. It is sad to say that in all likelihood, many families have the children involved in multiple sports so the husband and wife can tolerate each other.

Listen to the story of 'Ken and Jackie' from William P. Farely's *Gospel-powered Parenting:*

> *Ken and Jackie were sincere parents. But their sincerity was their problem. They loved their children. In fact, they loved them too much. The oldest son was a talented athlete. He excelled on the local U16 soccer team. Because the team practiced during the dinner hour, the family stopped eating meals together. They had been in the habit of praying and reading the Bible after meals. This also ended.*
>
> *Their daughter was an exceptionally talented ballerina. Her lessons were expensive. Ken and Jackie couldn't afford them and tithe at the same time. We will resume tithing when she graduates, they rationalized.*
>
> *Soon the family was traveling to weekend soccer tournaments. Most were on Sundays, so church attendance became increasingly sporadic. Slowly, their social world began to revolve around the other soccer parents rather than their church family. Although their son and daughter attended the church youth functions, soccer and ballet always came first. At age sixteen, their daughter began to audition with professional ballet troupes in distant cities. Soon the family was traveling to her weekend auditions.*
>
> *Eventually the children went off to college. Within a few years they had both quit attending church. They forgot God. They threw themselves into their real interests, athletics and dancing. Ken and Jackie were deeply troubled.*[6]

If God places a priority on marriage, it is no stretch to say that His followers should too. We could also say that if God places

---

6. William P. Farely, *Gospel-Powered Parenting*, pp. 31-33.

such a priority on marriage, the world, our sin, and the Devil will be working hard to undermine it. Marriage is the institution God uses to teach us about His love for the church (Eph. 5). If the Bible is stressing this, we need more Christians standing up for their marriages. Christian marriages shouldn't be spent carting kids around all week and weekend long. The marriage should drive the calendar of the Christian household, not sports.

I am fearful that far too many Christians have lost sight of this. They have simply jumped into the youth sports culture without much discernment. Because of this, their marriage has suffered. Perhaps the sports practices and games are actually giving some couples time together by offering a sort of babysitting, and if that is the case, great! If not, brothers and sisters, please take a stand for the institution of marriage and cut back a bit from a child-dominated home.

'God-centeredness is the willingness to make our marriages more important than our children. Our children are with us for only eighteen to twenty-five short years. Most marriages have as many years without children as they do with. It is a big mistake to put your children ahead of your marriage.'[7]

The Original Team

One of my favorite memories of any sport I played for any season is the broad-focused memory of being a part of a team. It is something special. Each of you is working towards a goal. You have spent countless hours together in blood, sweat, and tears. A team forges some of the best and most significant relationships. A family does and should function like this. Truth be told, a family should be greater than this. In fact, you hear many teams say that they are more than a team, *they are a family*.

While God places emphasis on the institution of marriage, He also places an emphasis on family. By God's grace, it is through marriages that He often blesses couples with a family.

---

7. Ibid. p. 36.

As we noted, our pre-teens and teens are dealing with enormous issues and challenges. Challenges dealing with pornography, homosexuality, transgenderism, abortion, rape, molestation, eating disorders, stress, depression and suicide. Children must know that they can talk to their parents about these issues, but they won't if there has been no investment in these relationships.

Talking about some of these most difficult issues is the fruit of hours and hours of conversation about other issues from childhood. Survey after survey reveals that children still see their parents as their primary influencers.[8] However, surveys are also showing that teens latch on to their peers when their parents aren't around. Teens start to value the opinions of their peers when they are the ones talking to them about sex, drugs, politics – topics that should be discussed in the home.

Christians must place a premium on family time together. Meals together are an intimate setting and a must for a family to thrive. Not too long ago, I saw a parent and child eating fast-food in the front seat of their car before an athletic competition. I was sad because I knew there were other family members absent from that equation, not to mention a table. While I know there is nothing wrong with eating food on-the-go, it saddens me to know it has now become normative to share a meal on the road with a divided family. I am not saying there aren't times when it's appropriate to share a meal with a divided family. However, family meals with a complete family seem to be a growing rarity of our modern times.

In her book, *The Secret Thoughts of an Unlikely Convert,* Rosaria Butterfield draws attention to the harried lifestyles the sport's culture often creates and how that impacts the home, as well as,

---

8. According to the National Study of Youth and Religion, the single most important influence on the religious and spiritual lives of adolescents is their parents. The best social predictor of what a teenager's religious life will look like is to ask what her parents' religious lives look like. Kenda Creasy Dean, *Almost Christian: What the Faith of Our Teenagers is Telling the American Church.* (New York, NY: Oxford University Press, 2010), p. 203.

the broader culture. 'It would make such a bigger impression on our children's future, I suggest, to be calling off most of their persistent sports idolatry to enjoy family dinner at home and practice the "love of strangers" with such guests. Today's children know little or nothing of such an approach to community. And our churches wonder how to reach the lost. Reach them for what?'[9]

From many discussions I've had, it seems that families do not sit down at the table together that often anymore. Family meal times are now a novelty to most. It is very likely that many children are growing up without an understanding of a family meal. There are children who simply haven't witnessed these moments.

Please know that I say all of this with the belief that family is among the chief idols in the church. We must be cautious of turning our families into idols, but we must also place the biblical importance God's Word places on the family. To do this, we must tell coaches, teams, and others 'no' in order to say 'yes' to the family.

Even though there is a distinction with those who share our last name, I also want us to consider our brothers and sisters in Christ as our family. In Matthew 12:46-50 we read, '*While [Jesus] was still speaking to the people, behold, his mother and his brothers stood outside, asking to speak to him. But he replied to the man who told him, "Who is my mother, and who are my brothers?" And stretching out his hand toward his disciples, he said, "Here are my mother and my brothers! For whoever does the will of my Father in heaven is my brother and sister and mother".'*

Jesus broadened our understanding of family. We all have the name 'Christian' and that's deeper than the last name Perritt, for example. Thinking about the single people in our lives, they are a part of this family and sadly they can often be neglected in the church. Christians must prioritize the church in our life – not just attendance on Sundays, which is vitally important, but sharing life together. Helping the single mother

---

9. Rosaria Butterfield, *The Secret Thoughts of an Unlikely Convert: An English Professor's Journey into the Christian Faith* (Pittsburg: Crown & Covenant, 2014), p. 153.

who's barely keeping her head above water, as an example. Loving each other, serving each other, rebuking each other.

Yes, there is a distinction and instruction Scripture gives us on family and there is responsibility parents have in raising the children God has given them, but let's also see how God broadened our understanding of family.

Missing Practice

I once heard a story about a man converted while serving a life-sentence in prison. His conversion occurred by his privately reading God's Word. No one preached to him, no one taught him, no one evangelized him. He opened up God's Word, read it, and was convicted over his sin, repented and placed his faith in Jesus Christ. God's Word is indeed 'living and active' (Heb. 4:12).

My point is that God saves people in any way He chooses. He can use other humans, animals – like donkeys – (Num. 22:21-39), He can raise up rocks to worship Him (Luke 19:40), He can use whatever means He wants because He's God. There are extraordinary means that He uses, but He also uses ordinary means, means like the Word, prayer, and church. As I've heard someone say, church is Christians practicing worship before we get to heaven. It's a practice we don't need to miss.

As I've already said, church attendance saves no one. There isn't a Sunday school or church roster in heaven that Peter is checking when you arrive, 'Uh oh, the fall was a pretty bad season for you, John. Why did you miss so many services?!' No one is saved by their church attendance. That being said, *there have been plenty of people saved through attending church.* People have been saved by going to Sunday school. It's not in their actual attendance, it's in the Spirit's working through God's Word and His people.

God uses the preaching of the Word to save and sanctify sinners – it's His design. While we aren't saved by our church attendance, why would we not want to worship the One who saved us? Why do we view church attendance as a chore? In our attempt to properly place salvation by grace through faith in Jesus, have we swung the pendulum too far in our abhorrence of a legalistic mindset towards church attendance? To say it another way, church attendance is a big deal. Skipping it is, too.

'Those most serious about communing with Christ will be diligent to share in fellowship with other Christians,' says, Kevin DeYoung, 'The weakest Christians are those least connected to the body. And the less involved you are, the more disconnected those following you will be. The man who attempts Christianity without the church shoots himself in the foot, shoots his children in the leg, and shoots his grandchildren in the heart.'[10]

Yes, we are not saved by going to church, but it is vital to our Christianity. More importantly, when we know our children are young, have not grasped the faith, and are unconverted, why in the world would we miss another opportunity for them to hear the truth of God's Word? Sunday morning worship should be a priority for our families because hell is a real place, and we want to ensure they love their King.

In a sermon, Kevin DeYoung brings some helpful thoughts on church attendance and youth sports. In many ways, I feel like this is *the* question Christian families wrestle with. 'How do you prepare for Sunday on Saturday?' says DeYoung:

> *Is it wrong to watch football on Sunday? I don't think you could say so from Romans 14 or Colossians 2. But, is it wrong to make the focal point of a resurrection Sunday the watching of football or the playing of youth soccer … I think so. Parents have to face these difficult questions … Without laying down the sort of law that Paul would forbid us. I think it's within the parameters of Scripture to certainly exhort you to think about what sort of example we are setting for our children with regards to the Lord's day and to worship. Is there a more important habit that you can ingrain in your children than the habit that says, 'We go to church on Sunday.' There are few things I am more thankful for getting from my mom and dad … Sunday is the day the Lord has given you to attend to your soul … if we were physically sick we would go to the doctor, we would check the Internet, we would call our insurance company … whatever I have*

---

10. Kevin DeYoung, *The Hole in Our Holiness.* p. 132.

to do to get well ... we spend so much time during the week in soul-shriveling activities and God says, 'Here is a day for your soul to breath and to grow and to be nourished ... we love our kids and we want them to excel and give them all the opportunities ... the best thing you can do for your kid is to teach them the importance of Lord's day worship Sunday after Sunday after Sunday.[11]

Even among those who skip church for sports related activities, there are those who still consider themselves consistent church attenders. Thom Rainer says, 'An active church member fifteen years ago attended church three times a week. Now it's three times a month.'[12] Culture has redefined what an 'active member' of church is.

Matt Fuller discusses this in light of Hebrews 10:24-25 (NIV), 'And let us consider how we may spur one another on towards love and good deeds, not giving up meeting together, as some are in the habit of doing, but encouraging one another – and all the more as you see the Day approaching.' Fuller states, 'I meet lots of people who call themselves "regulars" at church; but their definition of regular is about one week in three. That's not what the writer of Hebrews means. If we're committed to spurring one another on – if we regularly think through how we might do that – then we'll need to see each other very regularly.'[13]

It is true that parents can turn their child's salvation into an idol. We can wrongly stress over it, have anger directed towards God if we sense that our children are unconverted, or guard them from the world thinking this will save them. Nevertheless, it seems that the majority of Christians today give little thought to their child's salvation. It seems that many parents are too

---

11. See https://christcovenant.org/sermons/the-reason-for-rest/; last accessed March 2018.

12. Thom S. Rainer, *Discouragement in Ministry – Rainer on Leadership* #086, January 2, 2015. https://thomrainer.com/2015/01/discouragement-ministry-rainer-leadership-086/; last accessed February 2018.

13. Matt Fuller, *A Time for Everything: How to be Busy without Feeling Burdened* (Epsom: Good Book Company, 2015), p. 101.

easily convinced their children love Jesus because they know some Bible answers. Many of these parents seem oblivious to false professions of faith.

The Bible is filled with stories of those who did not persevere to the end, those who seemed to have an outward faith, but turned away at the end of their life. Judas, maybe the most familiar, shocked the disciples by his turning away from Jesus.[14] While church attendance does not guarantee a child's perseverance, continual exposure to God's Word will most likely strengthen it. Again, it is a means of grace God uses in the life of a Christian.

Having this perspective on church should change the light-hearted attitude many families have towards Sunday morning worship. Parents, God has graciously given you stewardship responsibility over the soul of your child. Why not make every effort to bring them to the Word, not only for their salvation, but for them to worship their Maker, their Redeemer, their Friend?

Among the strongest opponents of church these days are youth sports activities. I can tell you that there are plenty of students who are absent an entire semester from Sunday school and church. There are also those families who travel every weekend for a semester but make the effort to attend churches other than their 'home' church. While this is good and admirable, these families are absent from fellowship with their local congregation. They are absent to welcome visitors in their own church. Their voice is one less voice in their local congregation to join in the chorus. Their hands and feet are absent to assist in service to that congregation. Their absence is a big deal; it should be.

The Need for Half-time

As mentioned earlier, there are numerous purposes half-time can offer a sport. Not only does half-time give players an advantage to rest, it also gives them the opportunity to strategize and makes changes to their play. It gives cheerleaders time to rest. Band

---

14. For more on Judas see *What Would Judas Do?* by John Perritt (Ross-shire: Christian Focus Publications, 2017).

members have an opportunity to perform. If the game is broadcast over television or radio, it gives the announcers an opportunity to rest and take a break. Half-time also serves as an intermission for fans who don't want to break away from the live action. At its foundation, half-time serves as a brief pause for those involved in a game – this includes those watching from home.

What Christians need to see is that God has designed rest to be a part of creation across cultural contexts. As Adrian Reynolds says, 'Sleep is part of our created humanity, a good gift from God to be treasured and enjoyed; an earthly picture of a spiritual reality.'[15]

Not only does this rest manifest itself halfway through many sports, it does so at the completion of the game. There's a rest throughout the week for athletes to better perform for game time. Most coaches won't have their players practice hard prior to the game because they need to be well-rested. Anyone who has a job knows they also have time off. They have daily breaks away from their profession; i.e., 8 a.m. to 5 p.m., for example. Even doctors that are on call have moments where they rest.[16] It is our rest that fuels our productivity, whether that's on or off the field. To this point, there's a coach who claims that if a student is underperforming, it is most likely due to their lack of sleep.[17]

When it comes to our student athletes, they need some rest. Studies show that middle and high schoolers still need around eight hours of sleep, but – in my twelve plus years of student ministry – I don't think I've met students who get that much sleep.

---

15. Adrian Reynolds, *And So to Bed...: A Biblical View of Sleep* (Scotland, UK: Christian Focus, 2014), p. 10.

16. 'Doctors, they say, with less than six hours' sleep between procedures make double the rate of surgical errors.' Adrian Reynolds, *And So to Bed...: A Biblical View of Sleep* (Scotland, UK: Christian Focus, 2014), p. 15.

17. Jeff Jordan is the athletic director and head football coach of Garland High School in Garland, TX. He says, when dealing with students struggling to build strength and gain weight, he asks about their diets and training routines and follows up with, 'How many hours of sleep are you getting?' http://www.dallasnews.com/life/healthy-living/2013/09/02/the-secret-to-teen-athletes-success-might-be-their-sleep; last accessed February 2018.

According to the National Sleep Foundation, only 15 per cent of students are getting the needed eight to ten hours of sleep a night.[18]

Athletically, students have maxed out the hours they could possibly give in any given day in order to guard from injury. According to an abstract presented at the American Academy of Pediatrics conference last fall, adolescent athletes who slept eight or more hours each night were 68 per cent less likely to be injured than athletes who regularly slept less.[19] Academically, the remaining hours are filled in with class time and homework – homework that's often completed in the wee hours of the night (or morning, depending on how you think of it).

The rest that does come for these young minds and bodies is often from church-related things. If students are literally maxed-out when it comes to academic study and athletics, the spiritual is often the first to go. After all, most spiritually related things don't impact the resume all that much. More often than not the students that do show up to ministry-related events, like Sunday school or mid-week Bible studies, struggle to stay awake, and that is understandable.

Simply put, our students are maxed out and are not taking advantage of the gracious rest God offers. To be quite blunt, the youth sports culture is not structured to allow for much else besides that sport. To the coaches, there isn't much else that matters. If a student misses practice, they're benched. If a student is a star, they are exploited.

You see, the sports culture has taken on the characteristics of the professional culture. In many cases, youth sports exceed the amount of time collegiate athletes give. Not all of this is the coach's fault. The parents must take some of the blame. The coaches are hired to win games and if they don't, they're fired.

18. https://sleepfoundation.org/sleep-topics/teens-and-sleep; last accessed February 2018.

19. Mary Jacobs, 'The secret to teens' athletic success might be their sleep' September 2013. http://www.dallasnews.com/life/healthy-living/2013/09/02/the-secret-to-teen-athletes-success-might-be-their-sleep; last accessed February 2018.

Therefore, the pressure to win is on the coach, and a coach knows they need to practice in order to win. That being said, these student athletes' bodies need to rest.

Alan Williams was a basketball walk-on at Wake Forest University. He reflects upon some parental intensity after refereeing a game at the age of seventeen. 'That particular incident,' says Williams, 'leads me to address an overriding problem in youth sports today. Parents need to lighten up. I look back at my friends who were the stars in elementary and middle school. They had a lot of talent, but their dads coached every single one of their teams. Their parents forced their sons to go to personal trainers and sent them off to as many basketball camps as possible during the summer ... A dad shouldn't know that his fourth-grade son is shooting 74 per cent from the free-throw line.'[20]

While there is much debate over God's command to Sabbath, let's simply say this: our God is a gracious God who expects His children to rest. He is not a slave-driving God, like Pharaoh during the period of Exodus. He is a God who tells His children to rest. We should rejoice in this truth. In Scripture this ultimately points to our eternal rest in Jesus, but it also means that we need to take a nap.

To quote Reynolds again, '[T]he willingness to lie down and sleep is itself an expression of trust and faith in a sovereign God.'[21] Reynolds is telling us that we can rest because God is a God who neither sleeps nor slumbers and He's caring for His children. 'God's sleepless character is the very reason that the good gift of sleep He gives to His children can be both treasured and enjoyed.'[22]

God did all the work in salvation, so we can rest in that truth. We also need daily rest from work. We need to rest after

20. Alan Williams, *Walk-On: Life from the End of the Bench* (Austin: New Heights, 2006), p. 137.

21. Adrian Reynolds, *And So to Bed...*, p. 26.

22. Ibid. p. 45.

sprinting, weight-lifting, jumping, throwing. Human bodies were designed to rest, and much of our rest is experienced through the Sabbath day. God graciously gave us a day to rest. Sadly, many Christians see this through eyes of legalism, when in fact this rest is anything but legalistic. You see, legalism requires work, rest has everything to do with grace. No doubt Christians can shoehorn this into a legalistic mindset, but let's see a gracious God calling His followers to rest.

I firmly believe that a greater emphasis upon rest will fuel the spiritual lives of families. Fewer will be depressed, stressed, and medicated. Students will be healthier in every sense of the word – emotionally, physically, and, most importantly, spiritually. Let's steward our children by allowing them to rest.

As I stated at the beginning of this chapter, much of what I tried to assert in terms of boundaries is rooted in God's Word. I attempted to place emphasis on what His Word clearly places emphasis on and attempted to be less clear where there tends to be debate. Some may assert that there is vagueness to some of what was said and much of that is intentional. Christians must be cautious of making hard and fast rules where Scripture does not.

While I know that I made some strong assertions at some points in this chapter, I did try to be cautious. I want to be cautious to guard from guilt, but I do want to foster diligence since we are called to diligently impress the faith on to our children. As it has been said, 'Children are the living messages we send to a time we will not see.'[23] What sort of message of faith are we leaving behind – through our children's lives – to a generation we will not see?

---

23. Neil Postman, *The Disappearance of Childhood* (New York: Random House, 1994), p. xi.

CHAPTER 12

END OF REGULATION

Let me tell you something kid; everybody gets one chance to do something
great. Most people never take the chance, either because they're too scared,
or they don't recognize it when it spits on their shoes.

— 'THE BABE,' *The Sandlot* (1993)

*B*RIAN Regan is a comedian who's made me laugh numerous times throughout the years. In one of his standup routines he relays the story of a certain doctor's visit. As he's leaving the visit, he states that the doctor, rather nonchalantly, says, 'Oh yeah, no more dairy.' Regan says, 'That's like saying, "By the way, no more happiness".'

Some of you reading this may think I'm the same way. Some joy-robbing author attacking your favorite pastime. Let me be as transparent as I know how to be; sometimes I've wondered that about myself as well. John, how could you question something so many enjoy? How could you critique something you, yourself, love? There are Christian athletes who use their platform for God's glory; why question something that gives them a platform? Trust me, I have had these inner battles throughout the time I have spent considering this subject. Still do. It is not overstatement to say that I have been haunted by the content of this book. The haunting notions have not stopped there however. Am I wrong? Am I being closed-minded in my assertions? Are my conclusions too strong? Has my own sin blinded me to God's grace through sports? Even though I encouraged you to 'keep it between the ditches,' I'm sure there are times I've veered too far to one side or the other. The finished product in your hand is not free of error. I am confident that many will find things to criticize that will result in concessions on my part.

Although my conclusions most certainly contain fault, I am confident of one thing that lies before you: *sincerity*. I have sought to be as vulnerable, critical, truthful, and transparent as I can. I know that some will see this as brash and lacking in grace. Where I have been a bit strong, it has been birthed from a heart of sincere concern for the future of the church, a heart that is not free from sin, but one that strives to cling to God's Word in any assertions that are made.

Parents, some of you have been blessed with phenomenal athletes. They may be able to run, jump or throw better than anyone on their team or the state you live in; maybe they are among the elite that will play on the next level. It could be true that they will one day be featured on primetime television and admired by fans across the globe.

But, the truth I continue to come back to is eternity. Who cares about any athletic ability our children have if they don't have Christ?

Timothy Paul Jones asks, 'What does it profit our child to gain a baseball scholarship and yet never experience consistent prayer and devotional times with us, the parents? What will it profit our child to succeed as a ballet dancer and yet never know the rhythms of a home where we are willing to release any dream at any moment if we become too busy to disciple one another?'[1]

I have already said that our children can have Jesus and sports, but Christ is clear that we cannot serve two masters. Matthew 6:19-24 tells us that we are to be laying up treasures in heaven. If that is the teaching of Christ, we can be confident that our sin desires the exact opposite, that is, treasures on earth.

The praise of man is so enticing, and having our child receive the applause of the crowd drives much of the youth sports insanity, as previously stated. It lures many to receive their reward

---

1. Timothy Paul Jones, *Family Ministry Field Guide*, p. 103.

on this earth instead of the next life. Eternity is before us and our children, and I fear that sports has blinded us to the eternal far more often than we like to admit, or are even consciously aware of at times.

Our world is a beautiful one. A world with joy, love, and recreation God has graciously bestowed. Yet, it is a world broken by the devastating effects of sin. It is a needy world. A world littered with poverty, sexual perversion, and death. It is a world that is in desperate need of the gospel of Jesus Christ. While God graciously gives us enjoyment in sports even though we sinned against Him, our recreation can blind us to the need that's all around.

Sports can make us laugh, have deep joy, and sincere community. Sports and recreation, I believe, will also be enjoyed in the next life.[2] Sports are great, but, as is the case with many good things, they are often used as a means to numb us to many realities in life.

Sometimes this 'numbness' can be a good thing. The husband who is stuck working for an overly, critical, difficult boss looks forward to some Saturday football to get his mind off the difficulties. The tensions parents have with their child can be put on hold as they watch her talents on the field. The cancer diagnosis of a mother weighs heavy on a family, but the time spent at the fields is a welcome balm – a balm that brings true physical, spiritual, and emotional nourishment in a dark season.

From a bad job, to strained relationships, to weighty issues like cancer, God gives us sports. Not to be *the* answer, but to move us to worship the One who is the answer to all of life's problems. Sports are a blessing bestowed by a gracious God, but we must be practicing biblical stewardship of sports so that parents and students are not missing the God behind the gift. I am not guiltless in my lack of stewardship of sports.

---

2. In Donald Macleod's *A Faith to Live By: Understanding Christian Doctrine*, (Christian Focus, 2015) he claims that Christians will have glorified bodies possessing athleticism undreamed of.

While I've spent the majority of this book reiterating the belief that sports are indeed a grace, Christians need to be discerning enough to see how quickly and easily sports can become idolatry in their life. As Lincoln Harvey says, '[T]he church should remain vigilant. Sport will always be a perfect arena for idolatrous self-worship. It easily slips into the pagan (self-) worship of nature.'[3] Christians must remain vigilant to have discerning hearts in the sphere of sports. John Piper says: '[W]e will be shaped by the world without intentional efforts not to be.'[4]

I feel the constant need to pull back and remind of us of the good of sports. I feel the need to do that, because most will not read this book if I do not. Now, however, I want to focus on those who have a heart that would reject a book that too heavily critiques sports. I want you to prayerfully consider your heart and ask how the world has possibly shaped your heart in the sports culture. If you get offended by any critique of sports, chances are sports have become enthroned in your life. I do not say this to be overly harsh; rather, I say this as a strong, biblical warning of idolatry.

When parents are organizing their schedules around the team, funneling exorbitant amounts of money into their sports, minimizing serious injuries incurred through youth sports, and allowing the spiritual discipleship of their child to fall by the wayside, they have missed the God of the Bible and are forging a new god. There may be some who say they are enjoying sports as a grace, but it looks more like an abuse of grace.

Here are some good diagnostic questions to assist us in discerningly engaging with the sports culture:

- How often is your child immersed in God's Word?

---

3. Harvey Lincoln, *A Brief Theology of Sport* (Eugene, OR: Cascade, 2014), p. 103.

4. C. J. Mahaney ed., *Worldliness: Resisting the Seduction of a Fallen World* (Wheaton, IL: Crossway Books, 2008), p. 12.

- Does your child have any time to have a devotional life?

- Is there a family devotional time or meal time you have together?

- How often are you missing Lord's Day worship or rushing out of worship to get to the fields?

- Are sports controlling your calendar or is church and service controlling your calendar?

Scores of Christians these days can be found screaming on the sidelines instead of singing hymns. They can be studying the skills of their child and where they need improvement, but when it comes to studying theology that takes too much effort. As Matt Chandler says:

> *I think you should know your Bible a little bit better than you know your football team. I think that's basic. People say that they're not a good reader but can give me football statistics. They're brilliant when it comes to 18-year-olds throwing a ball, but they can't devote themselves to the Bible.*[5]

At a lunch a few years back, I sat with a father discussing youth sports. While this father was often at the soccer fields on Sundays instead of the church, he lamented about his embarrassment to me. His comments were, 'When I'm at the fields on Sunday during church, I see half of our members there. They wave to me, but I'm embarrassed. I don't want to be seen out there.' The embarrassment waned as it became a normal practice for the family to be absent from church and present on the field.

I believe the message of this book is an important message for the church. That should not be too surprising, as I've just

---

5. Matt Chandler, 'A Shepherd and His Unregenerate Sheep,' *Desiring God*, 2009 Pastor's Conference, http://www.desiringgod.org/messages/a-shepherd-and-his-unregenerate-sheep; last accessed February 2018.

written an entire book on the topic. When I entered The Southern Baptist Theological seminary and began thinking about my thesis, I almost instantly knew it would be on this topic. In many ways, I feel like my fifteen plus years of youth ministry were preparing me to write this book.

I mentioned earlier that much of this book was written out of sincerity, but the sincerity is broader than what I formerly said. It extends to those around me. I sincerely don't want to hurt the families I've ministered alongside. I sincerely don't want this to affect the way my own children are treated. I sincerely don't want to sever relationships over this topic. I don't want to cause division or guilt. I hope this book doesn't move people to feel attacked. I sincerely hope I do not heap shame upon parents that often feel shamed for their parenting.

At the same time, I sincerely believe this is a message the church needs to hear. It is a message pastors need to communicate to their congregations. It is a message youth workers and fellow parents need to be communicating. It is a message some will be unwilling to hear. It is a message that will be misunderstood. But it is a message about which I cannot continue to remain silent, because I worship a Savior who is to be treasured above all else. Come to think of it, that's a good place to end: the Gospel.

Regardless of where you come down on this entire issue – a negative or a positive view of youth sports – I'm confident Christians can agree on this. A Christian's involvement in sports is difficult. It is not a black and white issue. It is very complex and confusing.

It is an issue that causes guilt – sometimes unfairly and other times accurately. It is a grace that is sinfully worshiped at times, yet at other times it is properly enjoyed. You see, sports is an issue just like anything else on this earth. It is an issue that gets complex when sinners are involved. If it didn't cause disagreements, anger, guilt, idolatry, or frivolousness of time, money, and energy spent, then we wouldn't need Jesus ... but we do.

Through the fog of confusion over youth sports involvement, we can see the cross of Jesus Christ, the empty tomb, and the horse and its Rider coming soon. Jesus worshiped His Father perfectly. Lavished a love on His Father that never waned. He was patient, loving, kind, gracious, and compassionate to all those He came into contact with.

The truth is, Jesus loves stubborn people like you and me. Jesus died for a people that deny Him more often than they realize. Jesus earned righteousness, paid the penalty of His children's sins, and rose from the grave out of love for His Father and love for a people that would give more glory to sports than they often give to Him. He did all of this for a people who fail continually in their stewardship of time and money. Who fail to steward their bodies and souls like they are called. If we were not helpless failures we would not need a Savior, but we are … so we do.

Any guilt you've felt over this discussion on the youth sports culture, please take it to the cross and rest in the redemption Christ purchased for you. The Gospel is good news for parents that fail in their parenting; parents who worship their children and neglect the church. But, as you take your guilt and shame associated with parenting to the cross, be sure and take your kids there as well.

APPENDIX 1:

DISCUSSION BEFORE A GAME

In order to impart a biblical worldview of sports to our children, here are some helpful questions and talking points to assist our children in keeping their mindset on eternity as they play this earthly game.

- Remember that your arms and legs, gifts and skill were given to you by God. Each game is a gift and an amazing opportunity.

- We are more concerned about your Christian character on the field than we are about winning. Be a Christ-like example to your teammates as well as the other team.

- Be cautious of your temperament on the field. Not only are your words and actions something you must be aware of, but your heart as well.

- You will be tempted towards pride, vanity, revenge, anger, and other emotions. Be in constant prayer over your heart – we will be praying for you, too.

- What ways do you think you'll be tempted to sin?

- (If your child is a star) Warn them about their arrogance. Work on ways to foster humility. Remind them that their identity is not found in being the star athlete and it can quickly be taken from them.

- (If your child sits the bench) Work on ways to encourage them to be a good teammate. Remind them that their identity is not found in being a star athlete.

- Sample Prayer: Heavenly Father, You are good and gracious in so many ways. Sports/recreation/games are one of the good gifts You give to Your children. Please help my son/daughter to honor You on the field today and be more focused on their Christian example than winning or losing. Help them to be reminded that they are Your child and a win or loss can never take that away. Help them to try hard, run fast, play tough, but guard their heart from sin. They will be tempted with so many emotions during this game. They will be tempted to say something or do something or think something that may go against what the Bible says is right and true. Please give them the strength of Your Spirit to walk in a manner worthy of Christ on this field/court/etc. It's in His name we pray. Amen.

APPENDIX 2:

DISCUSSION AFTER A GAME

For parents to remain faithful to disciple their children and impart a biblical worldview to their child, a post-game discussion will be a vital and helpful practice.

- What was the highlight of the game for you? If it was a certain athletic play, highlight the Creator behind the creation.

- What was the team highlight? Was there one moment that pointed to team unity and excitement? There's so much Christianity says about unity/fellowship, so be sure to highlight this aspect of sports. If it's more of an individual sport, discuss ways in which the spectators and athletes were unified.

- What was a discouragement that occurred on the field? Were there ways in which you sinned in thought, word, and deed, that you need to confess and grow in?

- If you lost, what do you think you learned from it? What are some things you could have done better? What are some things your team could have done better? Do you think your team 'deserved' to win? That is, did your team put forth a good effort or did the other team work for it more than you?

- What are you most thankful for in your performance? How do you think the Lord used you on the field?

- Did you thank your coach for the time and energy she/he put into this particular game? Were there decisions your coach made that you disagree with? Be sure and honor him/her even if you disagree, but know that it's okay to talk to us about possible disagreements.

- Sample Prayer for a Win: Heavenly Father, You are always good. Win or lose, nothing changes that. Today, we thank You for a victory. It is fun to win and it fosters a celebratory feeling among teammates. There is joy to be felt, but please remind us that this joy is temporary. There are other games and other seasons to be played, so this joy is very fleeting. Lord, we do pray for our opponents who lost and ask that you'd encourage them and that you'd use this loss to point them to ultimate joy in you. While we thank You for this joy, we ask that You keep our minds on eternity and the full joy that Jesus Christ accomplished for us. It's in His name we pray, Amen.

- Sample Prayer for a Loss: Heavenly Father, You are always good. It is never fun to lose a game, but that does not change Your love and care for Your children. Please teach us through this loss. Teach us humility and grow us from the bitter taste of defeat. We ask that You forgive us for particular ways in which we thought, spoke or acted on the field. Help us always to work hard, but to be a gracious loser and an example of Christ-like character even in defeat. Lord, we pray for our opponent as they celebrate victory. We pray that they would enjoy the taste of victory, but know that it is fleeting. I pray that this loss would help us see how temporal the joys of sport are and how sweet the promises of eternal life are through the finished work of Jesus, Amen.

APPENDIX 3:

A MESSAGE TO THE NON-ATHLETE

In all this talk about youth sports, what about the youth who don't like sports? The students who either 'didn't have what it takes' to compete or those who simply didn't find sports all that enjoyable? Well, to both I would say that there's more to life than sports. However, writing an entire book devoted to youth sports might seem like a contradiction.

With twenty-four-hour coverage devoted to sports, entire sports channels, team jerseys donned among children and parents alike, athletic teams and clubs at most schools, hundreds of fans in the stands, and millions of youth playing sports every year, it might seem like sports are the purpose to life.

A parent may quickly shrug this off by thinking, *Sports are fun, but we know there's more important things.* What about the ten-year-old mind and heart? Do they know? How do they process the exorbitant amount of time, money, and attention athletes and athletics receive? How do they understand that there is – indeed – more to life than the field?

I've witnessed firsthand, and heard parents, lament the fact that their child isn't athletic. As if this was some sort of birth defect or disease their children were diagnosed with. For the record, the lamentations of these parents were more focused on the ostracizing their children often received from their peers. At school, their child was seen as less valuable and less popular; resulting with a sense of worthlessness to their young heart and mind.

Could it be that we, as adults, have funneled too much time, energy, worth, concern, love, desire, and excitement into youth sports that we make children feel less valued when they're not the athlete? Are parents at fault here?

I've just spent an entire book passing along a biblical world-view towards athletics, so I hope you're walking away with some talking points to have with your child. One clear point I hope you make to your children is the fact that sports are a good and fun thing, but a child's worth and value is not found in that thing.

Parents, if you have a non-athlete or a child who wasn't 'good enough' to make the team, one of the most important truths your child must know is the love and acceptance they have from their parent. Communicate this clearly and often. 'We don't care if you're athletic. We love you and nothing will change that.' This is a message your child must consistently hear.

Secondly, and more importantly, they need to grasp their identity as a child of God. They need to know that this is the most important identity they can have. And, even if that doesn't seem to ease their pain as their young mind struggles to understand it, continue to communicate it to them. Pray it for them and teach it to them continually. They need to know that acceptance with God the Father is the only acceptance that matters and they have that through the finished work of Jesus.

While not making the team or being left out of a particular friend group due to sports will hurt children, maybe the Lord will use that pain to help your child let go of this world and cling to Him – the true Lover of their Soul. My intent isn't to be flippant in my dismissal of the pain a parent and child may receive from this – it's real and it hurts – but, this world is passing away and their life – sports included – will soon be over. If they are a true child of God, and at the end of all things will dwell with Jesus for eternity, being unathletic won't even be an afterthought.

BIBLIOGRAPHY

Altrogge, Stephen. *Game Day for the Glory of God: A Guide for Athletes, Fans, & Wannabes*. Wheaton, IL: Crossway, 2008.

Beale, G.K. *We Become What We Worship: A Biblical Theology of Worship*. Downers Grove, IL: IVP Academic, 2008.

Bergler, Thomas E. *The Juvenilization of American Christianity*. Grand Rapids: Eerdmans, 2012.

Berkhof, Louis, *A Summary of Christian Doctrine*. Carlisle, PA: The Banner of Truth Trust, 1960.

_____ , *Systematic Theology*. Grand Rapids, MI: William B. Eerdmans Publishing Company, 1932.

Boyd, Brady. *Addicted to Busy: Recovery for the Rushed Soul*. Colorado Springs: David C. Cook, 2014.

Brown, Raymond. *The Message of Hebrews: Christ Above All*. Downers Grove, IL: InterVarsity Press, 1982.

Burk, Denny. *What is the Meaning of Sex?* Wheaton, IL: Crossway Books, 2013.

Carter, Joe. *NIV Lifehacks Study Bible: Practical Tools for Successful Spiritual Habits*. Grand Rapids, MI: Zondervan, 2015.

Challies, Tim. *Sexual Detox: A Guide for Guys Who Are Sick of Porn*. Adelphi, MD: Cruciform, 2010.

Chantry, Walter. *Call the Sabbath a Delight*. Carlisle, PA: The Banner of Truth Trust, 1991.

Clark, Chap. *Hurt: Inside the World of Today's Teenagers.* Grand Rapids: Baker, 2004.

DeYoung, Kevin. *Crazy Busy: A (Mercifully) Short Book about a (Really) Big Problem.* Wheaton, IL: Crossway, 2013.

_____ . *The Good News We Almost Forgot: Rediscovering the Gospel in a 16ᵗʰ Century Catechism.* Chicago: Moody, 2010.

Kenda Creasy Dean, *Almost Christian: What the Faith of Our Teenagers is Telling the American Church* (New York, New York: Oxford University Press, 2010)

Edgar, Brian. *Time for God: Christian Stewardship and the Gift of Time.* The Evangelical Review of Theology (2003) Vol. 27, No. 2.

Elkind, David. *The Hurried Child: Growing Up Too Soon Too Fast.* 3ʳᵈ ed. Cambridge, MA: Perseus Books, 2001.

Fadling, Alan. *An Unhurried Life: Following Jesus' Rhythms of Work and Rest.* Downers Grove, IL: InterVarsity, 2013.

Farley, William P. *Gospel-Powered Parenting: How the Gospel Shapes and Transforms Parenting.* Phillipsburg, NJ: P & R, 2009.

Fuller, Matt. *Time for Every Thing? How to Be Busy without Feeling Burdened.* Purcellville, VA: Good Book, 2015.

Gibbs, Chad. *God and Football: Faith and Fanaticism in the SEC.* Grand Rapids: Zondervan, 2010.

_____ *Love Thy Rival.* Glencoe, AL: Blue Moon, 2012.

Grabill, Stephen. *The Church's Call to Steward God's Mission in the World.* The Gospel Coalition, August 19, 2014. https://www.thegospelcoalition.org/article/the-churchs-call-to-steward-gods-mission-in-the-world

Harvey, Lincoln. *A Brief Theology of Sport.* Eugene, OR: Cascade, 2014.

Higgs, Robert J., and Michael Braswell. *An Unholy Alliance: The Sacred and Modern Sports.* Macon, GA: Mercer University Press, 2004.

Hoffman, Shirl James. *Good Game: Christianity and the Culture of Sports.* Waco, TX: Baylor University Press, 2010.

Hyman, Mark. *Until It Hurts: America's Obsession with Youth Sports and How It Harms Our Kids.* Boston: Beacon, 2009.

Jones, Mark. *Organized Sports on Sundays?* Reformation 21 (2014).

Jones, Timothy Paul. *Family Ministry Field Guide: How Your Church Can Equip Parents to Make Disciples.* Indianapolis: Wesleyan, 2011.

Keller, Timothy. *Counterfeit Gods: The Empty Promises of Money, Sex, and Power, and the Only Hope that Matters.* New York: Penguin, 2009.

_____. *Every Good Endeavor: Connecting Your Work to God's Work.* New York, New York: Riverhead Books, 2012.

_____. *Ministries of Mercy: The Call of the Jericho Road.* Phillipsburg, NJ: P & R, 1989.

_____. *The Prodigal God: Recovering the Heart of the Christian Faith.* New York: Penguin, 2008.

Kluck, Ted. *The Reason for Sports: A Christian Fanifesto.* Chicago: Moody, 2009.

Kluck, Ted, and Kristin Kluck. *Household Gods: Freed from the Worship of Family to Delight in the Glory of God.* Colorado Springs, CO: NavPress, 2014.

Köstenberger, Andreas J. *God, Marriage, and Family: Rebuilding the Biblical Foundation* 2nd Edition. Wheaton, IL: Crossway Books, 2010.

Ladd, Tony, and James A. Mathisen. *Muscular Christianity: Evangelical Protestants and the Development of American Sport.* Grand Rapids: Baker, 1999.

Lawrence, Michael. 'Biblical Theology and Identity.' 9Marks, (2014).

Lloyd-Jones, Sally. *Thoughts to Make Your Heart Sing.* Grand Rapids: Zonderkids, 2012.

Mahaney, C. J. *Worldliness: Resisting the Seduction of a Fallen World.* Wheaton, IL: Crossway, 2008.

_____. *Don't Waste Your Life.* Wheaton, IL: Crossway, 2011.

Mueller, Walt. *The Space Between: A Parent's Guide to Teenage Development.* El Cajon, CA: Youth Specialties, 2009.

_____. *Youth Culture 101.* El Cajon, CA: Youth Specialties, 2007.

Myers, Kenneth A. *All God's Children and Blue Suede Shoes: Christians & Popular Culture.* Wheaton, IL: Crossway, 1989.

Packer, J.I. *Concise Theology: A Guide to Historic Christian Beliefs.* Wheaton, IL: Tyndale House Publishers, Inc., 1993.

Parsons, Burk. 'Not Lords, Stewards.' Ligonier Ministries, (2011).

Payne, Tony. *How to Walk into Church.* Youngstown, OH: Matthias, 2015.

Pipa, Joseph A., Jr. *The Lord's Day.* Fearn, Scotland: Christian Focus, 1997.

Peace, Martha, and Stuart W. Scott. *The Faithful Parent: A Biblical Guide to Raising a Family.* Phillipsburg, NJ: P & R, 2010.

Postman, Neil. *The Disappearance of Childhood*. New York: Vintage, 1994.

Prince, David. *In the Arena: The Promise of Sports for Christian Discipleship*. Nashville, TN: B&H Publishing Group, 2016.

Rigney, Joe. *The Things of Earth: Treasuring God by Enjoying His Gifts*. Wheaton, IL: Crossway, 2015.

Roberts, Vaughan. *Transgender*, UK: The Good Book Company, 2016.

Sande, Ken, with Tom Raabe. *Peacemaking for Families: A Biblical Guide to Managing Conflict in Your Home*. Carol Stream, IL: Tyndale, 2002.

Sisemore, Timothy A. *World-Proof Your Kids: Raising Children Unstained by the World*. Fearn, Scotland: Christian Focus, 2007.

Tebow, Tim, with Nathan Whitaker. *Through My Eyes*. New York: Harper Collins, 2011.

Treat, Jeremy. 'More than a Game: A Theology of Sport.' *Themelios* 40, no. 3 (2015): 392-403.

Tripp, Paul David. *Age of Opportunity: A Biblical Guide to Parenting Teens*. Phillipsburg, NJ: P & R, 1997.

_____ . *Sex and Money: Pleasures that Leave You Empty and Grace that Satisfies*. Wheaton, IL: Crossway, 2013.

Williams, Alan. *Walk-On: Life from the End of the Bench*. Austin, TX: New Heights, 2006.

Williamson, G. I. *The Westminster Confession of Faith: For Study Classes*. Phillipsburg, NJ: P & R, 1964.

Wolters, Albert M. *Creation Regained: Biblical Basics for a Reformational Worldview*. Grand Rapids: Eerdmans, 2005.

John Perritt

WHAT
WOULD
JUDAS
DO?

Understanding faith through
the most famous of the faithless

What Would Judas Do?

Understanding faith through the most famous of the Faithless

JOHN PERRITT

In this 31-day devotional, John Perritt looks at the life of Judas—the experiences he had living with Christ, the things he would have seen and heard, and his terrible final resolve. This is a book which challenges our hearts and makes us feel uncomfortable—and leaves us with tears of praise, wondering at the amazing salvation which we have in our Christ.

We have more in common with history's greatest traitor than we may care to admit. But by reflecting on the failures of Judas we can better see how we can become more like Jesus.

Joe Carter
Editor at The Gospel Coalition and Author of *NIV's Lifehacks Bible*

The contrarian in me loves this—a look at Jesus through the eyes of His betrayer. And a look at our own relationship with Jesus through exploring theirs.

Barnabas Piper
Author of *The Pastor's Kid*, *Help My Unbelief*, and *The Curious Christian*

Some will find this book to be a needed warning, others will find it deeply comforting, but all who read it will be pointed to Christ's finished work.

Jason Wredberg
Senior Pastor, First Baptist Church, Watertown, Wisconsin

978-1-7819-1809-8

JOHN
PERRITT

YOUR **DAYS** ARE NUMB3RED

A CLOSER LOOK AT HOW

WE SPEND OUR TIME

& THE ETERNITY BEFORE US

Your Days are Numbered

A Closer Look at How We Spend Our Time & the Eternity Before Us

JOHN PERRITT

Wasting time might not seem like a big deal to some, except for the fact that our time really isn't ours, but God's. Not only that, but it is a limited resource. You can be the richest person in the world and you still can't buy more time.

If we want a heart of wisdom, according to the psalmist, we must number our days. *Your Days are Numbered* takes a biblical look at the way in which we spend our time to cultivate this mind–set of seeing each day as a vital opportunity to live for the glory of God.

Of all the gifts God gives to us, few are more precious and few are more fleeting than the gift of time. Your days are numbered and you are responsible to faithfully steward each one of them for the good of others and the glory of God. This book will teach and encourage you to make the most of the time God gives you.

Tim Challies
Blogger at www.challies.com

... *Your Days Are Numbered* succeeds in addressing it with simplicity and practicality. If heeded, John Perritt's common sense proposals grounded in scriptural principle will enable us to 'redeem the time'.

David Strain
Senior Minister, First Presbyterian Church, Jackson, Mississippi

978-1-7819-1744-2

Christian Focus Publications

Our mission statement –

STAYING FAITHFUL

In dependence upon God we seek to impact the world through literature faithful to His infallible Word, the Bible. Our aim is to ensure that the Lord Jesus Christ is presented as the only hope to obtain forgiveness of sin, live a useful life and look forward to heaven with Him.

Our books are published in four imprints:

CHRISTIAN
FOCUS

Popular works including biographies, commentaries, basic doctrine and Christian living.

CHRISTIAN
HERITAGE

Books representing some of the best material from the rich heritage of the church.

MENTOR

Books written at a level suitable for Bible College and seminary students, pastors, and other serious readers. The imprint includes commentaries, doctrinal studies, examination of current issues and church history.

CF4•K

Children's books for quality Bible teaching and for all age groups: Sunday school curriculum, puzzle and activity books; personal and family devotional titles, biographies and inspirational stories – because you are never too young to know Jesus!

Christian Focus Publications Ltd,
Geanies House, Fearn, Ross-shire,
IV20 1TW, Scotland, United Kingdom.
www.christianfocus.com
blog.christianfocus.com